Nonviolent Lives

*People and Movements Changing the World
Through the Power of Active Nonviolence*

Ken Butigan

Pace e Bene Press

Nonviolent Lives

People and Movements Changing the World
Through the Power of Active Nonviolence

Nonviolent Lives: People and Movements Changing the World Through the Power of Active Nonviolence
Published by Pace e Bene Press
To order individual or bulk copies,
Visit www.paceebene.org, Call 510-268-8765, Email info@paceebene.org

Library of Congress Cataloguing-in-Publication Data
Butigan, Ken 1953-
Nonviolent Lives: People and Movements Changing the World Through the Power of Active Nonviolence / Ken Butigan
ISBN-13: 978-0-9978337-0-6
ISBN-10: 0-9978337-0-X

Library of Congress Control Number: 2016917104

Cover and design layout: Ryan Hall
Cover photo by Thomas C. Davis, Wilmington, Delaware — From the Campaign Nonviolence Week of Actions March for Peace in Wilmington, DE, September 2014

For Leah Toyomi Butigan –
May these nonviolent lives
inspire your own

Contents

Foreword by Medea Benjamin

"How do you keep going in the face of such terrible realities?" I am constantly asked. "How can you stop from becoming depressed and giving up?"

One of the best antidotes to despair is reading about the lives of people who never gave up, visionaries who believed in the impossible despite the overwhelming obstacles they faced; visionaries who never resorted to violence despite the violence unleashed against them; visionaries who turned the impossible into the inevitable.

As *Nonviolent Lives* so beautifully depicts, it is the fortitude, gumption, perseverance and determination of visionaries that has propelled major leaps in justice for the human family, leaps such as women's suffrage, civil rights and gay marriage. But these visionaries don't appear out of thin air. They are products of the moments they live in and the movements they embody and embrace.

What I so appreciate about *Nonviolent Lives* is that author Ken Butigan, whose own life has been dedicated to nonviolent change, provides such a graceful and delicate balance between the individual protagonists and the mass movements they are part of, between transformative lives and nonviolent, transformative movements. Without a base, without a mass movement, without a support system, visionaries are simply dreamers. It takes a movement to transform dreams and aspirations into realities.

Butigan is also careful to provide another critical balance. Some of the stories are about historic, larger-than-life figures such as Martin Luther King and Dorothy Day, or people like Wangari Maathai whose massive tree planting in Kenya was recognized with a Nobel Peace Prize. Such figures are certainly inspiring, but hard to emulate. They often seem too brilliant, too determined, too bold for us to aspire to. But other, equally compelling stories in *Nonviolent Lives* are the stories of unsung heroes who many

1

readers will encounter for the first time, people who more of us might relate to. These include courageous "interrupters" who intervene to stop the killing on the streets of Chicago and creative graffiti artists whose shocking images force the public to wake up and take notice of glaring injustices.

These unsung heroes are people I encounter around the world. They are Central American campesinos organizing nonviolent land takeovers to wrest unused land from wealthy elites with armed militias. They are African locals trying to stop big, destructive dam projects or abusive mining companies, risking their lives in the process. They are indigenous community leaders struggling to keep their ancestral lands and rivers and forests. They are young activists in our inner cities fighting guns and police violence, or environmentalists in our rural towns fighting coal mines and fracking.

Whether still living or long gone, famous or unknown, domestic or international, young or old, the figures we read about in *Nonviolent Lives* have a common core. They struggled without weapons; their "arms" are empathy, compassion and love. At a time of so much violence in the world, these examples of nonviolent lives and movements are indeed the best antidote to despair. They give us hope, meaning and inspiration for our own lives and for our collective, global future.

Introduction

Successful social change hinges on many factors: strategic thinking, creative action, serious training, critical mass, and the capricious accidents of history. But transforming society requires more than applying the tenets of organizing or the vagaries of big picture probabilities. It is a thoroughly human process that ultimately turns on the gumption of people and their intangible power. Dramatic movements can inspire and spur us to action—but we are also deeply nourished by examples of ordinary human beings whose relentless determination so often lies at the heart of social transformation. If they can do this, we find ourselves saying, why can't I?

Those of us who long to change the world would do well to enroll in an ongoing course that could be called "Nonviolent Lives for Powerful Change 101." In this class we could study—and be vicariously mentored by—a series of characters whose lives illuminate the qualities and values that the long-distance run for social change requires. We would pour over the stories of lives transforming the world, transforming others, and transforming themselves.

This course would include such figures as Mohandas Gandhi and Dr. Martin Luther King, Jr., but even more to the point it could zoom in on the often unsung women and men who form the backbone of nonviolent change, like those who never miss a meeting or who quietly go about the business behind the scenes of energizing one movement after another.

For years I've thought about keeping a running "Chronicle of Gratitude"—a volume of reflections on the virtually endless stream of women and men for whom I am thankful. Those I have known. Others I will never meet. People who have made an impact on my life and the lives of others by being who they are—and by all the ways they have struggled for change, sparked new awareness, shared their depth, or have otherwise placed the gifts of survival and transformation in our trembling hands.

This book combines both impulses. These pages offer you a course featuring nonviolent lives, and the transformative movements they inspired and built, for whom we can all be grateful. It is both a book-length class from which we can glean many lessons for the way forward and a potentially contemplative experience through which we can savor, and be deeply thankful for, the example of sisters and brothers who have plunged into the challenging and powerful work of deep change.

The backdrop to this book is both personal and social.

First, the personal. I have been fortunate to participate in numerous nonviolent struggles for change ever since the moment in the early 1980s when I plunged into the global movement for nuclear disarmament. Not long after that, I went to work full time seeking to end the Reagan administration's wars in Central America. I was a lead organizer of the Pledge of Resistance, a movement where tens of thousands of people pledged to engage in nonviolent civil disobedience or other forms of nonviolent dissent to prevent an invasion of Nicaragua and to end military intervention throughout the region. There is some evidence that this movement succeeded, against long odds, in meeting many of its objectives.

After this, I went to work for Pace e Bene Nonviolence Service, a training and movement-building non-profit organization founded by the Franciscan Friars of California. Pace e Bene (meaning "Peace and All Good," a phrase of St. Francis of Assisi) has facilitated over 800 trainings and workshops in the vision and toolbox of nonviolent change, and has built or actively supported a number of movements, including resisting the U.S. invasions of Iraq and Afghanistan, supporting East Timor's independence from Indonesia, challenging systematic discrimination against homeless people in San Francisco, California, and resisting the U.S. government's policy of torture. For over a quarter of a century I have been actively involved in these efforts in collaboration with many committed and creative friends and colleagues.

In the following pages, soundings from this personal journey make an appearance—not by presenting a comprehensive memoir but as occasional windows on specific moments of movement-building that can offer us lessons and perspectives today as we face new and different challenges.

But more than my own journey, this book highlights key campaigns, movements and personalities committed to re-shaping the world for the well-being of all.

This book comprises an honor roll of activists who have committed their lives to nonviolent social change, some of whom are now no longer with us, including Vincent Harding, Wangari Maathai, César Chávez, Narayan Desai and Ed Dunn. I join my voice with many others in celebrating the powerful legacy each has left in their wake.

This book offers an overview of some of the issues that have beset us over the past few years. Virtually all of these pieces were written between mid-2011 and mid-2014. In most cases, I sought to reflect on what was trending—what was most immediately on the social radar at the time—but also the connection between the challenges of the present and the past out of which they grew. Hence the number of pieces that latch on to an anniversary of a key event from the history of social change, always with an eye to seeing what light our history can shed on our contemporary fix.

In preparing this volume, it was intriguing to review even such a short span of time—the last several years—and see the wide variety of events and ideas that captured our attention, with some still urging us forward, others faded from view, and still others having actually succeeded—for example, the movement to stop the Keystone XL Pipeline.

The stories in Part 1— Nonviolent Lives in Action—single out a particular cast of characters in the great drama of transformation. These are people whose lives have sparked the imagination of many of us to live more humanly and nonviolently and to take on the difficult but powerful work to change our world. In Part 2—Nonviolent Lives Up Close—I reflect on agents of change whom I have come to know over many years. I am deeply grateful for what they have taught me about a world where the default is the well-being of all. In Part 3— Nonviolent Lives Working Together—we turn to movements: a few of the many powerful initiatives where many catalysts for change have joined hands to move us forward.

These pages offer a meditation on powerful people and effective movements who can teach us about building a culture of peace, justice and nonviolence. Though the selection is not comprehensive—many change-makers and movements from the recent past have not made it into these pages—but, taken together, they provide an overview that is multi-dimensional, as if they all comprise a larger movement, a movement of movements, for a more caring and cared for world.

By using the term "nonviolent lives," I do not mean that the women and men profiled here are perfect beings or have perfectly embodied the vision of nonviolence. The nonviolent life is a continual struggle with violence and injustice, including one's own. What I mean by using this phrase is that those chronicled in these pages have committed themselves to the challenging and powerful process of relieving suffering and contributing in large and small ways to building a better world by activating the tools of creative nonviolent change.

Virtually all of these essays were first published by *Waging Nonviolence*, a critically important website that daily serves up analysis and news on the power of nonviolent change. I am grateful to Eric Stoner, Nathan Schneider, Bryan Farrell and Jasmine Faustino for their tireless work chronicling nonviolence in action, and for permission to publish these pieces in this book.

Three of these pieces were not published by *Waging Nonviolence*, including the first, "César Chávez: Pilgrimage of

Nonviolence," for which I have reached back over two decades to a time I was fortunate enough to be part of a bi-cultural team facilitating nonviolence workshops with Latino/a youth in the place where Chávez lived and worked. I am very grateful to all those who made these explorations of the nonviolent life so rich and powerful.

I am also thankful for many other lives who have taught me so much, including my friends at Pace e Bene. Veronica Pelicaric, Ryan Hall, Rivera Sun, John Dear, Kit Evans-Ford, Dariel Garner, Louie Vitale, Sr. Janet Ryan and a host of Pace e Bene and Campaign Nonviolence Associates comprise the present, life-giving circle. There are many other expanding circles – the growing Campaign Nonviolence movement; the Nonviolence and Just Peace movement sparked by a powerful Vatican conference attended by change-agents from throughout the world; the faculty and students at DePaul University's Peace, Justice and Conflict Studies Program; and the Catholics for Nonviolence movement at the Chicago Archdiocese. And many others. Thank you all.

May the lives and movements lifted up in the following pages inspire us. And may we inspire others by also living the courageous, risky and beautiful life of active nonviolence for the well-being of all.

PART ONE:

Nonviolent Lives in Action

We are constantly being astonished these days at the amazing discoveries in the field of violence. But I maintain that far more undreamt of and seemingly impossible discoveries will be made in the field of nonviolence.

— Mohandas Gandhi

Nonviolence means avoiding injury to anything on earth in thought, word or deed.

— Mohandas Gandhi

At the center of nonviolence stands the principle of love. To retaliate with hate and bitterness would do nothing but intensify the hate in the world. Along the way of life, someone must have sense enough and morality enough to cut off the chain of hate. This can be done only by projecting the ethics of love to the center of our lives. Agape love means understanding redeeming good will for all men and women, an overflowing love which seeks nothing in return. It is the love of God working in the lives of men and women. When we love on the agape level we love men and women not because we like them, not because their attitudes and ways appeal to us, but because God loves them. Here we rise to the position of loving the person who does the evil deed while hating the deed he does.

— Martin Luther King, Jr.

1

César Chávez: Pilgrimage of Nonviolence
March 31, 1994

It is my deepest belief that only by giving our lives do we find life. I am convinced that the truest act of courage...is to sacrifice ourselves for others in a totally nonviolent struggle for justice.

— César Chávez, on breaking an historic 21-day fast

I think nonviolence is a very natural way of doing things, and violence is highly out of the ordinary.

— César Chávez

I am firmly convinced that nonviolence cannot exist only in books or on the seminar level on our university campuses, but it must exist in the flesh. I have always believed that people are the most important element we have. We must put flesh into our nonviolence rather than simply talk about it.

— César Chávez

We can change the world if we do it nonviolently. If we can just show people how they can organize nonviolently, we can't fail. Nonviolence has never failed when it's been tried.

— Cesar Chavez

People equate nonviolence with inaction, with not doing anything, and it's not that at all. It's exactly the opposite... Nonviolence is action. Like anything else, though, it's got to be organized... If we can just show people how they can organize nonviolently, we can't fail. It has never failed where it's been tried.

— César Chávez

11

Tell everyone to engage in public action for peace and justice. Public action, public action, public action! That's the solution!

— César Chávez

Our strikers here in Delano and those who represent us throughout the world are well trained for this struggle. They have been under the gun, they have been kicked and beaten and herded by dogs, they have been cursed and ridiculed, they have been stripped and chained and jailed, they have been sprayed with the poisons used in the vineyards; but they have been taught not to lie down and die nor flee in shame, but to resist with every ounce of human endurance and spirit. To resist not with retaliation in kind but to overcome with love and compassion, with ingenuity and creativity, with hard work and long hours, with stamina and patient tenacity, with truth and public appeal, with friends and allies, with mobility and discipline, with politics and law, and with prayer and fasting.

— César Chávez

The land is rich and flat and endless. As I leave the highway and travel east under the brilliant moonlight, I am aware with each passing mile that we are traversing holy ground.

This is California's San Joaquin Valley, the source of much of the nation's food. This fact alone would make it a sacred place. But the holiness of this region goes beyond its bounty. This land has been consecrated by the lives of those who make that abundance possible, those who have worked and lived and died here—many of them poor, many of them moving from field to field like pilgrims on an endless pilgrimage.

Most importantly, this land has been irrevocably blessed by a process set in motion decades ago: a decision by poor and powerless people to join together in nonviolent resistance to demand their dignity. *We are human beings*, they announced at that time, *and we oppose intolerable working conditions, low pay, and the lack of basic respect.* They then backed this declaration by launching the United Farm Workers (UFW), a movement co-founded by César Chávez that used nonviolent strikes, boycotts, fasts, education and public mobilization to spark a process of far-reaching social change.

As we drew closer to Delano—the site of Forty Acres, the original headquarters of the movement, where I would be part of a bi-cultural team leading a four day retreat on "César Chávez's Nonviolence"—I was increasingly cognizant that we were entering a specific place (like those other places in the Deep South, in India, in the Philippines, in South Africa, and in many other places) where the human spirit had confronted violence and injustice with the relentless persistence of active, creative, and empowering nonviolence.

Shortly after César Chávez's unexpected death in April 1993, members of the Franciscan Province of Saint Barbara, which had worked closely with the UFW throughout the 1960s and 1970s, decided to honor this prophet of nonviolent change by holding a series of workshops on his work and vision for Latina and Latino youth from throughout California. Now, in February, 1994 I was traveling to Delano to join three other long-time workers for justice and peace in leading the first workshop: Leonardo Vilchis, an organizer at Dolores Mission, a Jesuit parish in East Los Angeles that has been addressing gang violence with nonviolent strategies; Olga Islas, the director of religious education at Our Lady of Guadalupe Church in San Jose, which had once been Chávez's home parish; and Br. Ed Dunn, OFM, the director of the province's Social Concerns Committee.

Retreat participants included forty women and men from youth groups associated with Franciscan parishes and ministries in Sacramento, San Francisco, Oakland, Palo Alto, San Jose, the San Joaquin Valley, and Los Angeles. In addition, we were joined for the entire weekend by fifteen of the original UFW strikers, known as *huelgistas* (*huelga* is Spanish for "strike").

13

During our days together, the stories, insights and testimonies of these founders of the movement touched us deeply. At times, we felt that we were observing, and participating in, the transmission of a tradition of resistance and hope from cultural elders to the next generation.

Over these days together, we gained more acquaintance with the broad outlines of the history of this struggle—including the protracted table grape strikes and boycotts waged over these three decades and other specific vignettes from that history.

For example, one *huelgista* told us that it was a regular practice of the county sheriff to give large helpings of non-union grapes to the jailed strikers and, rather than being provoked, they would set the tray of grapes aside and begin to pray!

On a more serious note, they shared with us how, after two picketers were killed during the 1973 strike, the UFW ended the strike but then launched an international grape boycott, sending the *huelgistas* throughout the US and Canada to tell the story of the struggle, including the brutality they had faced, and to organize the next phase of the campaign.

Woven throughout the weekend were a series of nonviolence principles that César Chávez, echoing Mohandas Gandhi and Martin Luther King, Jr., articulated in interviews, in writings and in the crucible of action. These included:

- Active nonviolence is rooted in the fact that human beings are gifts from God.
- Active nonviolence is a way to be neither a victim nor an oppressor.
- Active nonviolence is a way to wage conflicts in a human way.
- Active nonviolence seeks to break the cycle of escalating violence.
- Active nonviolence is a simultaneous journey inside us and outside us.
- Active nonviolence is not weak.

- Active nonviolence mobilizes "people power."
- Active nonviolence seeks the truth of the situation and firmly holds onto it.
- Active nonviolence creates a situation powerful enough to challenge injustice and to continue as long as it takes to produce change.
- Active nonviolence does not seek to conquer the opponent but to overcome the injustice of the situation by creating a solution that takes into account the humanness of all.

After four days of presentations, small group discussions, role plays, videos from UFW history, reflection on our local contexts, and a series of very special moments—including a powerful ceremony at César Chávez's simple grave at La Paz, the current UFW headquarters in Keene, CA—we had a sharper understanding of the work of Cesar Chavez and the continuing work of the UFW to improve the living and working conditions of millions of people.

On Sunday evening, we closed our retreat with a moving religious service. During this experience of prayer and music, the *huelgistas* commissioned each participant to carry on the vision and work of César Chávez, marking this call by solemnly bestowing on each participant a tiny cross fashioned by *campesinos* (farmworkers) in El Salvador.

Six week later, we held a follow-up gathering with the retreat participants living in the San Francisco Bay Area. As we reflected on the meaning of the experience, one person after another shared a dramatic story about how they had used what they had learned in Delano to transform recent violent situations in the streets and in the workplace. They talked about breaking the spiral of violence through creativity, communication and active nonviolence.

As we left our meeting that evening, we savored the way that the vision and practice of César Chávez lives on in the lives of these young agents of change, who are putting the power of nonviolence into action in the gritty situations of their lives. In so doing they are making their own streets and spaces sacred.

2

Martin Luther King, Jr.: The Kingian Classroom

August 30, 2013

The ultimate weakness of violence is that it is a descending spiral begetting the very thing it seeks to destroy. Instead of diminishing evil, it multiplies it. Through violence you may murder the liar, but you cannot murder the lie, nor establish the truth. Through violence you murder the hater, but you do not murder hate. In fact, violence merely increases hate. Returning violence for violence multiplies violence, adding deeper darkness to a night already devoid of stars. Darkness cannot drive out darkness; only light can do that. Hate cannot drive out hate; only love can do that.

— Martin Luther King, Jr.

I plan to stand by nonviolence because I have found it to be a philosophy of life that regulates not only my dealings in the struggle for racial justice but also my dealings with people and with my own self.

— Martin Luther King, Jr.

In the midst of the high-wire tension of the civil rights movement, Martin Luther King, Jr. found time in his relentless schedule in 1962 to offer a semester course on social philosophy at Morehouse College in Atlanta. This was the first and only college class he ever taught.

Recently celebrating the fiftieth anniversary of the 1963 March on Washington, the media spotlight predictably focused on the power and ringing rhetorical heights of King's "I Have a Dream" speech. What the students at Morehouse experienced one year before the march, though, was a different King — one who may have as much to teach us today as the thundering speeches he delivered in Montgomery, Birmingham, Selma, and at the Lincoln Memorial in Washington a half-century ago.

17

King taught the Morehouse course after moving back to Atlanta from Montgomery to become a co-pastor at Ebenezer Baptist Church. He certainly had a national reputation as the spokesperson of the successful Montgomery bus boycott in the mid-1950s, but he had yet to lead the epochal Birmingham campaign, receive the Nobel Prize, or address 250,000 people on the National Mall. King was not yet an international icon for civil and human rights, and he did not project rock star status in the classroom.

As the handful of those who took this course uniformly report today, King's professorial style in the classroom was down to earth and geared toward getting his students to think. He was not interested in preaching or even lecturing, but rather opening space for a wide range of perspectives. One student, perhaps looking for oratorical fireworks, has even concluded that the course was a "little boring," though another — Julian Bond, who went on to become a civil rights leader and Georgia state legislator — contradicts this assessment. "I wouldn't call it boring. Not at all."

What made this class exciting for most of these students was its combination of rigorous study and the opportunity to learn the intricacies of social change — not only from a leader of the Montgomery campaign, but also from the fact that they were simultaneously involved in the civil rights movement themselves.

Virtually every student recalls how voluminous and demanding the reading assignments for the course were, including texts on or from Socrates, Plato, Aristotle, Mill, Rousseau, Hegel, Thoreau, Edgar Brightman (whose theories on personalism had deeply influenced King in graduate school), and Gandhi. But King wasn't looking for rote regurgitation or superficial agreement about the meaning of these ideas. He instead created an environment where the students grappled with these works and applied their insights to the challenges of creating a democratic, multiracial and nonviolent society.

Heavy though the reading was, the course was more than textual analysis. The Montgomery bus boycott campaign had been a paradigmatic example of a triumph of people power through which King unpacked and illuminated the vision of nonviolent transformation. At the same time, a flurry of organizing took place in Atlanta that year, including sit-ins at segregated stores. Some of the students helped organize these protests, which King supported as he could. This class on "social philosophy" both nourished, and was nourished by, the concrete challenges and opportunities of living nonviolent action.

It is known that Dr. King wanted to teach in a seminary after he retired from the presidency of the Southern Christian Leadership Conference. He never got the chance. That's what makes this class so precious and remarkable. By acclamation, his former students say that it had a profound impact on their lives and their vocations. Many went on to become brilliant agents of nonviolent change.

But maybe there is more to it than the immediate impact on the few students that enrolled. In December 1962, SCLC and others held a retreat to strategize about the next year's action campaigns. It was during this planning session that the movement committed itself to bring the struggle the following spring to Birmingham, which, with the repressive measures of Sheriff Eugene "Bull" Connor, was considered the most visibly racist city in the South. The movement's disciplined nonviolence would dramatically contrast with Birmingham's glaring violence and, the assembled organizers surmised, spark a moral crisis that could build support for landmark civil rights legislation. In fact, this proved to be the case.

It's impossible to establish definitively that King's teaching of the Morehouse course had a direct connection to the winter strategy on Birmingham. But it is tempting to think that the opportunity to reflect deeply on the Montgomery movement — and, in turn, to teach, convey and engage with its lessons — may have given King the space to both savor that victory and to contemplate the possibility of another even more far-ranging one. While the chance to teach as a visiting professor might have appealed to his long-dormant academic side — or even, as one student assumes, provided some much needed income — its greatest gift to King may have been the chance to grapple in a safe environment with the possibility of a new campaign, one nourished by great thinkers and by even arguably greater experience. In addition to the vision and toolbox the course provided the students, it may have provided King with the occasion to mull on what might come next. Perhaps the consummate activist recognized the need for an intellectual and spiritual shift, if only for a semester, to help translate the impossible into the inevitable.

Aside from the tangible results that may be traced to this brief, scholarly interlude, even more intriguing may be the image that this story conjures up: Dr. King as the *world's* teacher.

Montgomery in 1955 had not only been a city in crisis, it also served as a kind of classroom where a different and, ultimately, more effective wisdom was being taught. It was grounded in the unifying power of people refusing to cooperate with their own oppression and, conversely, betting on a dramatic power that was neither passive nor violent. Birmingham, Selma, Washington, Chicago — these were historic schoolhouses where Gandhian and Kingian lesson plans were improvised and distributed on the wind far and wide.

Over the past five decades the whole world has become King's classroom, with students virtually from every nation and culture imbibing the great ideas of nonviolent change that have shaped minds and hearts everywhere.

The small Morehouse College class in 1962 was not at odds with King's real work. It was emblematic of the power of transformative education to foster a movement. It was another form of nonviolent action. But it was also a stand-in for the broad movement of human liberation to whom the Civil Rights movement helped give new life.

Dr. King's course is still being taught. Innumerable movements and campaigns everywhere have cribbed his syllabus and gotten the class discussion rolling. For half a century people have been taking a seat, scribbling notes, and taking what they've learned into a world that desperately needs the lessons of active nonviolence for monumental change.

3
Dorothy Day: Nonviolence and Resisting the Rituals of Violence
June 16, 2016

To me, nonviolence is the all-important virtue to be nourished and studied and cultivated.

— Dorothy Day

On June 15, 1955 millions of people crowded into air raid shelters in cities from coast to coast as part of "Operation Alert," a Civil Defense test ordered by the U.S. government. President Eisenhower and thousands of members of the executive branch flooded into shelters outside Washington. In New York City the drill's scenario envisioned that a hypothetical hydrogen bomb had gone off. In the mock attack 2,991,280 New Yorkers were said to have been killed.

Dorothy Day wasn't willing to play along.

Day, the co-founder of the Catholic Worker movement, and nearly thirty others were arrested for refusing to go down into the fallout shelter in New York's City Hall Park. In a statement they explained that "the kind of public and highly publicized drills held on June 15 are essentially a part of war preparation. They accustom people to the idea of war, to acceptance of war as probably inevitable and as somehow right if waged in 'defense' and 'retaliation'... They create the illusion that the nation can devote its major resources to preparation for nuclear war and at the same time shield people from its catastrophic effects."

For decades, Day had refused to countenance war – and now was not going to throw her support behind what she saw as an effort to get buy-in for an ongoing nuclear regime promising either all-out destruction or a state of perpetual fear. To fall into line with this dress-rehearsal would be to foreclose on the possibility that there was an alternative to nuclear violence or numbing passivity. She was holding out for the nonviolent alternative, and decided to dramatize it in a city park above ground, deliberately skipping the descent into the limbo of huddled terror. She had better things to do—feeding the hungry, visiting the sick. She was all about what the Christian tradition called "the corporal works of mercy," and saw in war the corporal works of death, that spread hunger, that increase suffering.

For Day, war was both a practical and a deeply spiritual problem. It was organized suffering that called us to resist its destuction and to administer the salve of healing, to work relentlessly for peace, and to take nonviolent action to calm its monumental storm of confusion and pain.

This is why Day had opposed every war that came along— World War I, the Spanish Civil War, World War II. Korea—and now this lethal make-believe enlisting whole societies in the regimentation of the Cold War.

With Peter Maurin, Dorothy Day founded the Catholic Worker movement in the early 1930s. Day had converted to the Catholic Church and saw issues of war, peace and justice as "Catholic issues." Her politics were inextricably interwoven with her spirituality because it was incarnational. The God of love, she held, has passed through this world and entered our suffering flesh. Day believed that Christians are called to inculcate respect and the deepest values of the human spirit. Influenced by the philosophy of personalism, her spirituality of the incarnated love of Jesus, of voluntary poverty, and of compassion was the basis of Day's prophetic nonviolence, which she espoused right down the line.

In April 2016, some 85 of us from all parts of the world gathered at the "Nonviolence and Just Peace Conference" co-sponsored by the Vatican's Pontifical Council for Justice and Peace. We concluded the gathering by calling on Pope Francis to share with the world an encyclical on nonviolence, and to spread the vision and methods of Gospel nonviolence throughout the church. Such a gathering is barely conceivable without the unrelenting work Dorothy Day did to call her adopted church to nonviolence, a commitment that the US bishops acknowledge in their 1983 pastoral letter on nuclear weapons.

Day not only held that nonviolence was central to the message of Jesus, she believed all Christians were called to translate this belief into action. Hence her countless picket lines, marches, rallies and nonviolent civil disobedience actions that netted her stints in jail that she often regarded as opportunities for prayer and reflection.

Arresting Day and her colleagues that summery day in New York did not deter the civil defense protest. In fact, they seem to have spurred it on, as annual mobilizations attracted growing opposition year after year, until in 1962, nearly 2,000 people refused to take shelter, sparking the definitive end to compulsory participation.

What, we might ask, are the rituals of violence and injustice that Dorothy Day would call us to resist in our own time?

4

Ameena Matthews, Cobe Williams, and Eddie Bocanegra: Violence, Interrupted

August 18, 2011

At the heart of Gandhi's revolution was a new kind of hero: brave, but also compassionate; bold, but also empathetic; powerful, but also unarmed. For millennia, traditional heroism had been fueled by the implacable absolutism of the Us vs. Them script—"we are good, they are evil"—enforced by justified violence. Gandhi's new heroism-subverting hero—whom he called a *satyagrahi*, a practitioner of Soulforce—bet her life on challenging and dissolving this ceaselessly reinvented and endlessly lethal dividing line.

"The Interrupters," a documentary from director Steve James and producer Alex Kotlowitz, vividly dramatizes this gamble in the midst of a culture of extreme youth violence on Chicago's South and West Sides. The film is an account of the haunting terror of seemingly inescapable gang conflict that is continually threatening to spin out of control—and that often does.

What sets this sobering account apart, however, is that it settles neither for ineffectual hand wringing nor a more traditional criminal justice perspective, including prosecution and incarceration as the solution to gang violence. Instead, it tracks over the course of a year a trio of "violence interrupters" – Ameena Matthews, Cobe Williams, and Eddie Bocanegra –who, like Gandhi's *satyagrahis*, are nonviolent first responders intervening in numerous disputes on the streets that threaten immediate carnage but also could touch off a larger war.

These and other interrupters are part of CeaseFire, an innovative nonprofit organization that "intervenes in crises, mediates disputes between individuals, and intercedes on group disputes to prevent violent events." The interrupters "know who to talk to, who has influence, and how to de-escalate a situation before it results in bloodshed."

CeaseFire touts what it calls a public health approach that seeks to prevent violence "on the front end" through interruption, intervention, risk reduction, and changing norms and behaviors. On the front lines are the interrupters, who have street credibility, rooted in years on the street and often long prison sentences for gang-related activity. Here is what Ceasefire says are the results of its model:

> CeaseFire launched in West Garfield Park, one of the most violent communities in Chicago in 2000 and was quick to produce results reducing shootings by 67% in its first year. CeaseFire's results have since been replicated more than 18 times in Chicago and throughout Illinois and has now been statistically proven by an extensive, U.S. Department of Justice funded, independent three-year evaluation. This evaluation scientifically-validated CeaseFire's success in reducing shootings and killings by 41% to 73% and demonstrated a 100% success rate in reducing retaliatory killings in five of the eight communities examined. The Model has been replicated more than a dozen times nationally and has two international sites in Iraq.

In June 2009, U.S. Attorney General Eric Holder, Jr., head of the Department of Justice referenced CeaseFire as an example of "a rational, data-driven, evidence-based, smart approach to crime – the kind of approach that this Administration is dedicated to pursuing and supporting." The John Hopkins Bloomberg School of Public Health conducted a subsequent evaluation of the Baltimore-based CeaseFire replication with initial results consistent with earlier Department of Justice evaluation findings and the University of Kansas demonstrated a 38% reduction in homicides for the first CeaseFire zone in Kansas City.

The Interrupters, however, does not dwell on these lofty results or analyses. Instead, it relentlessly takes us into the up-close immediacy of street-level battles and the ways CeaseFire's Interrupters engage these volatile and unpredictable situations, often with a combination of deep listening; confrontation; improvisation (including the offer to take an angry gang-banger to lunch, which he unexpectedly accepts); a worn wisdom that shows in their faces as they listen to the parties and weigh their next move; and a gritty, down-to-earth suasion rooted in their street cred. They've been there, and they know the outcome is often lockup or the cemetery.

The narrative effectively interweaves riveting real-time incidents or vignettes—a peace summit after the savage killing of a high school student; a tense funeral; a trip to the hospital where a CeaseFire supervisor visits with the first Interrupter to be shot in the line of duty—with the moving biographies of Ameena, Cobe and Eddie and their own difficult journeys of transformation and the day-to-day choice, against all odds and sometimes even their better judgment, to keep at it.

There are numerous cases in the film where they stay the course, even when the results seem miniscule or uncertain—as in the example of the mother and two sons who are in different gangs and who have deep fractures between them. Cobe persistently, but carefully, keeps opening doors, and gradually it seems that they decide to slide through them together, however tentatively.

But then there is the case of 18-year-old Lil' Mike who summons the gumption to apologize to the owners of a barbershop he had robbed a few years before, and now is a CeaseFire Interrupter working with youth. The scene, mixing Lil' Mike's forthrightness with the barber owner's anger, truth-telling, lack of sentimentality, and gesture of reconciliation, is jaw-droppingly moving. From many angles the film makes the point that both violence and nonviolence hinge on a subtle dance between an individual's journey, the abiding challenges of interpersonal relationships, and the larger narrative of the community's story and history.

There is a short but intriguing debate in the film about the larger impact of CeaseFire's approach. One of the Interrupters calls it a Band-Aid, while the director says that the broader project of structural change—including job creation and new community resources—itself depends on this kind of violence reduction.

Aside from these perspectives, it is possible to discern in this initiative an emerging anti-violence movement and potentially a broadly based movement for nonviolent social change. Ameena, Cobe, Eddie—and the many others featured in the film, including the people they are working with and supporting on the street—may become the leaders of an inclusive project that invites people from all sides of the line to turn from cycles of violence to building powerful movements struggling for economic justice and human rights.

The work of the Interrupters offers to all of us a clear and detailed example of how nonviolent change works. It is not passive, weak, ineffective, naïve, simplistic, or utopian. It is not perfect. It can be courageous, intentional, messy, creative, and able to re-weave the web a little bit at a time.

We have much to learn from this startling project.

5

Jonathan Little: Peacemaking
Circles as a Way of Life

September 13, 2012

"Four friends of mine were killed this summer," Jonathan Little tells a group of college students visiting Precious Blood Ministry of Reconciliation, a kind of peace zone in Chicago's Back of the Yards neighborhood. The young man's voice is somber but composed, as if he has taken the full measure of this abyss of suffering. He has decided that it's his duty to honor the dead by methodically pushing on with the work — the quest, really — of finding a way out of the storm of violence that bears down on the young in the precincts of poverty and institutionalized racism on the South Side of Chicago.

While he was still in high school, Jonathan came to Precious Blood and found something that went beyond the typical responses to the wave of violence engulfing his community. Instead of ineffectual moralizing, edifying utopian optimism or the punitive sledgehammer of the law, this project — housed in a nondescript building only yards from the border separating one gang's territory from another — takes a different tack: reweaving the web of life torn by crime and punishment.

Precious Blood is bent on reconciliation, and has launched a raft of creative projects to help make this a reality: theater arts, community mural painting, rituals of hope and healing, and mentoring that connects adults with youth transitioning out of the Cook County Juvenile Detention Center. There is the Arts of Peace Center, where participants express themselves and their reality through drawing, rapping, video production and building websites. These efforts sometimes become experiments in feeling one's way into a new story — visually, dramatically, poetically, digitally and relationally — that often opens up options that didn't seem to be there before.

Nowhere is the importance of a transformed story more alive than in the flurry of Peacemaking Circles that Jonathan and others lead virtually on a daily basis at the center. A Peacemaking Circle is a practice of restorative justice that seeks an alternative to the traditional approaches of the criminal justice system. It seeks to address and repair the harm that has been done to the victim and the community, but also to not give up on the perpetrator. It does this, as the ministry's website says, by reaching out to the victim, the wrongdoer, and the community to create a safe space where healing can begin and where people can find the support and encouragement needed to begin reconciliation. Precious Blood strives to be a resource to the community to find restorative ways to heal and rebuild after violence and conflict.

This approach stands in contrast to the official U.S. criminal justice system. While the courts often call on the victim to corroborate the charge, she or he is not offered means of healing. Peacemaking Circles offer a way to focus on healing for all.

This, however, is not easy. All parties have to be willing to touch the pain of violence. But the payoff is the possibility of creating a new collective story together, one rooted in "who we are" before getting to "what we did." As Precious Blood Ministry of Reconciliation director Fr. Dave Kelly, C.P.P.S., stresses, good does not come from tragedy, but "good can come out of us when we wrestle with disappointment and suffering ... good comes out of us in spite of the tragedy."

The power of the Peacemaking Circle lies in fostering an environment of respect, confidentiality, listening and truth telling. Composed of victims, wrongdoers and members of the community, it creates a container designed to hold anger, frustration, joy, truth, conflict, opposite opinions and strong feelings. The Peacemaking Circle process maintains that no one has the complete truth and strives to create a bigger picture. It does this using shared agreements, rituals, symbols and a talking piece held by the person who asks to speak. A Circle Keeper — what we otherwise might call a facilitator — guides the process.

There is no guarantee that transformation will take place. But one of the assumptions of Peacemaking Circles is that something good can come out of this process. In the years that Precious Blood has been facilitating Peacemaking Circles, it has seen this repeatedly. As part of an innovative arrangement with the courts in Chicago's Englewood neighborhood, a judge can offer some offenders the option of participating in a Peacemaking Circle at Precious Blood. Though Peacemaking Circles are not trials — which could re-traumatize the victim — under some circumstances the process can be held in lieu of a court trial. In other cases, some convicted offenders are offered a choice: sentencing by the court or participating in a Peacemaking Circle, which will focus on creating an outcome that is most healing and transforming for the victim, the wrongdoer and the community. The program has been so successful that six other judges in the area are considering offering this alternative in the near future.

Stories from the Peacemaking Circle process are riveting. A young man who robbed a house agreed to participate in a circle with the owner. By sharing their pieces of the truth in this safe environment, both experienced a shift in thinking and feeling. Now the young man has joined the basketball team the owner coaches.

Charged with battery, a young man agreed to meet with his victim. Through the Peacemaking Circle he learned that his victim was mentally challenged. This came as an unexpected and stunning revelation, and he felt compelled to repair the harm that he had done. He learned that the boy he had attacked liked video games, and he offered to teach him how to play some of his new games.

A drunk driver ran a red light and, colliding with another car, killed a man who left behind a wife and several young children.

The offender served a lengthy prison sentence. When one of the children was older, she wondered if the wrongdoer ever thought about the damage he had done. Approached about holding a Peacemaking Circle in this case, Fr. Dave contacted all parties and they agreed to take part. Their Peacemaking Circle lasted a day and a half. (Most are typically a couple of hours.) The widow and her children shared their wrenching pain and how all their lives had instantly and catastrophically changed. The offender shared his deep trauma at the horror he had inflicted and had thought about it every day since then. At the end of the circle, the children forgave the perpetrator. Their mother couldn't, but asked to stay in touch with the man. After six months of emailing, she, too, decided to forgive him.

Precious Blood Ministry of Reconciliation facilitates Peacemaking Circles for many groups. It holds regular sessions for family members who have lost children to violence, in English and Spanish. It holds weekly Peacemaking Circles for the larger community. It is often called in to schools.

And now it is going farther afield. It is about to train eight community organizations in the South and West Sides of Chicago to bring this process to their parts of the city. And Jonathan Little recently presented their work to an appreciative restorative justice conference in California. There is a growing community of Circle Keepers in Chicago and elsewhere, and they are slowly bringing this process into many settings.

While this process is beginning to get traction in some places, it is clear that the Peacemaking Circle's methods and assumptions would be transformative at every level of our society and our world. Sooner rather than later we must enter the age of restorative justice, and Precious Blood — where the circle is a way of living — is pointing us in this direction.

6
Indira Freitas Johnson: Changing the World One Ripple at a Time
March 14, 2013

In a world where, for some of us, our eyeballs are increasingly colonized by endlessly streaming Instagrams on the one hand and numbing corporate advertising that jams our public spaces on the other, the impulse to recover the enthralling power of the image — not to sell and distract but to startle, thrill, unnerve, reveal — can signal both a therapeutic and political act of nonviolent rebellion.

A troupe of artists are prying open the zone where images are neither commodified nor domesticated by editing the urban landscape with outsized photographs, capacious graffiti, and endlessly inventive paper and glue. Literally outsiders, they go public with bewildering visual moves aimed at stirring up a buzz of brain activity in the rest of us. While some of the work is overtly political, its power derives primarily from the way it reframes in a sudden and jarring way the physical and psychological architectonic jumble that most of us typically pass through without giving it a second thought.

The French photographer and guerrilla street artist JR ricochets around the planet wallpapering public spaces with powerful, monumental images of those he meets along the way, especially the rejected and despised. He changes up the social pecking order by wheat-pasting the portraits of those chronically relegated to the margins by literally framing them at the center of things. From the slums of Kenya to the favelas of Brazil he takes close ups that, as TED says, "are unguarded, funny, soulful, real, that capture the spirits of individuals who normally go unseen... Images of Parisian thugs are pasted up in bourgeois neighborhoods; photos of Israelis and Palestinians are posted together on both sides of the wall that separate them."

"Art can't change the world," JR says, "but art can change the way we *see* the world... and *then* we can change the world."

Another street artist who seems to share this attitude is Banksy. He spray-painted a series of images on the Israeli West Bank barrier, including a picture of kids chipping a hole through the wall and of a ladder going up and over it. His website offers a gallery of photos of his clever and thought-provoking street scenes strewn across cities in Britain and the United States, often ironically embellishing some feature of a wall or building that was there already.

When the Occupy movement streamed into the nation's plazas, parks and city squares a few years ago, many things were at work there, but one of them was a recovery and redefinition of public space, symbolizing a kind of resuscitation of the heart of civil society and literally bringing out into the open the concerns — about economic inequality, about the lack of participatory democracy, about the need for transparency — that had been gnawing at us while we were cooped up and overheating inside. Artists like JR and Banksy, who are revamping the urban terrain one wall or subway at a time, have similarly been driven outdoors to reclaim this space and to provoke the rest of us to dawdle — and perhaps even to ponder.

In Chicago there is a venerable tradition of street murals and graffiti (though the city also has a determined anti-graffiti effort). In this vein another public art project recently has been provoking double takes in the city's neighborhoods. Though Ten Thousand Ripples does not redefine public space with the same wild abandon of JR's built-environment canvasses or Banksy's effervescent but telling humor, it shares their determination to engage and provoke.

Some 30 statues of the Buddha — consisting of a serene and centered face emerging from the ground — have recently sprouted in Chicago neighborhoods regularly wracked with violence, including Pilsen, Back of the Yards, Little Village, Rogers Park, Uptown and North Lawndale. By late spring there will be one hundred. Created by artist and nonviolence educator Indira Freitas Johnson, Ten Thousand Ripples is collaborating with community-based organizations and schools throughout the city to inspire a conversation about peace and nonviolence.

Originally from Mumbai where her family was involved in spreading Gandhi's vision, Johnson had wanted to create public works that would speak of peace but not be traditional symbols like a dove, "which wouldn't surprise you or stop you in your tracks," as she told the *Christian Science Monitor*. While she is not a Buddhist, Johnson was drawn to the peace and calm the sculpture projected. The presence is "growing out of the earth," Johnson says. "Just like all of us... growing in our self-realization and our spirituality."

Some of the statues are 300 pounds. Others are smaller. I saw one at the edge of Loyola University Chicago in the Rogers Park neighborhood. It caught me off guard.

Part of the statue's power is this unexpectedness, but also the combination of familiarity and unfamiliarity it conveys.

In a very general and diffuse sense, U.S. popular culture has come to regard the Buddha as a symbol of peace and equanimity — based, in part, on a range of complex historical and cultural developments over the past century. Some of us, in addition, are aware of Engaged Buddhism, the movement inspired by Buddhist teacher and activist Thich Nhat Hanh — and spread by the Buddhist Peace Fellowship — who have taken Buddhist mindfulness practice into the world to resist war and injustice.

But none of this means we "get" these statues at first take. They resist easy categorization — partly because of the mysterious self-possession they radiate (a stately, composed visage half hidden by the earth), but also because they are not part of the traditional cultural codes most of us have been rooted in. This, I think, is one of the things that make them powerful. They are not immediately accessible. They force us to linger, to wonder — rather like the first Buddha whose enlightenment, and the peace and nonviolence that would flow from it, came out of prolonged waiting and stillness 2,500 years ago.

One could legitimately question whether a symbol dramatically outside the cultural expectations of a wide range of Chicago neighborhoods is more intrusive than inviting. We'll have to see if Johnson's impulse — to wrest Buddhist statuary from the contemplative garden or temple and, instead, plop it down almost randomly in the heart of a large American city — can indeed ripple out into awareness and even action. Nevertheless, like all nonviolent experiments, the growing flotilla of Buddhist witnesses for peace floating out into the sea of urban grit and conflict wagers mysteriously but resolutely that transformation is possible.

7

William Barber: Mobilizing Moral Mondays

August 15, 2013

"My arrest sheet says 'arrested for praying, singing and talking loud'—in other words, for preaching," thundered Rev. William Barber, a leader of the Moral Mondays movement in North Carolina, from the Wild Goose Festival's main stage last weekend in Hot Spring, NC. "I appreciate an audience like *this* so I can speak to an audience that's *not* like this."

Barber and hundreds of others from across the state—including a growing number of clergy—have been arrested at the capitol in Raleigh as part of a weekly, nonviolent protest since late April 2013, resisting the Republican-led legislature's wholesale attack on the state's social safety net and the infrastructure of civil society.

Beginning earlier this year the Republican super-majority has legislated severe cuts to public school funding (while approving a voucher program for private schools); terminated unemployment benefits for 170,000 North Carolinians (and slashing them for everyone else); rejected an expansion of Medicaid as part of the U.S. government's new health care policies; ended the earned income tax credit for working, low-income families; and made voting harder by restricting early voting, ending same day registration, prohibiting state-sponsored voter-registration drives, and creating stricter voter-ID requirements.

Over the course of thirteen Mondays, 960 people—from millionaires to the unemployed—have engaged in nonviolent civil disobedience to challenge the harsh new direction the state is taking.

While the protests have not derailed these new policies—the Republican-dominated legislature has been able to pass one bill after another—there are, at the same time, signs that this campaign is beginning to make headway. Barber, the president of the NAACP in North Carolina who is also a Disciples of Christ minister, quoted polls indicating that the Moral Mondays movement is now more popular in the state than the legislature. If the power and success of a movement ultimately flows from its ability to alert, educate, and mobilize the populace, this polling data may indicate that this effort is on its way to generating the people-power needed to create long-term change.

This week the movement entered its next phase. As the legislature finished its work in Raleigh at the end of July, campaign strategists swung their attention to the home districts of legislators across the state. Moral Monday actions are being organized each week in a different North Carolina city, and on August 27 this contemporary civil rights movement will commemorate the 50th anniversary of the March on Washington with simultaneous actions across the state. At the same time, the movement has begun to make the leap beyond North Carolina, with Moral Monday actions taking place this week in Chicago and Oakland focused on challenging policies aimed at dismantling hard-won gains for justice.

Rev. Barber arrived at the fourth annual Wild Goose Festival a few days after the second stage of the Moral Mondays movement was launched in nearby Asheville, where 8,000-10,000 people rallied. The festival—held this year near the North-Carolina-Tennessee border along the Appalachian Trail, surrounded by the Blue Ridge Mountains and the Pisgah National Forest—is an annual gathering "at the intersection of justice, spirituality, music" that draws people who are both progressive and Christian, though not everyone would claim these allegiances. There were over forty musical acts, scores of speakers, and a series of workshops held in a dozen covered spaces. About 2200 people attended. I was there with a nonviolence training crew from Pace e Bene Nonviolence Service, including Kit Evans-Ford, Jerica

Arents, and Marie Shebeck. We facilitated three workshops over as many days for several hundred people.

Most people camped—and all of us were drenched by the line of dramatic thunderstorms that periodically staggered through the mountains. On Saturday night the rain cleared long enough for a couple thousand of us to huddle at the main stage and be showered by the relentless intensity of River Runs North—a band comprised of young Korean-American men and women from LA—followed by the enduring energy and prophetic imagination of the Indigo Girls.

Everywhere we turned, presenters and participants were doing their best to help Wild Goose make good on its wager that justice has something to do with spirituality and creativity, but also nonviolence. If justice is the goal, the method is active nonviolence—this theme echoed through many presentations, including the exchange between Vincent Harding and Phyllis Tickle unpacking the perils and potential of the path of liberation ahead; Fellowship of Reconciliation organizer Lucas Johnson's meditation on "nonviolence as a spiritual discipline"; and author and activist John Dear's incisive exploration of Gandhi's principles. There was conversation on racism, food justice, and intersexuality. There were presentations on forgiveness, liberative parenting, and building inclusive community.

All of this came into sharp focus with William Barber's presence. There was an immediacy, breathlessness and monumental substance to the message he delivered from the multiplying front lines of a struggle that is local but at the same time national and global. His mission was not simply to report but to expand those lines, inviting every one of us to see that we are inescapably facing the same choice: will we lean our entire beings in the direction of a world that works for all of us?

With this piercing question Rev. Barber reframed Wild Goose. It was no longer only a festival. Even more than before it was a training ground and launching pad. He called on us to put into clear and unremitting practice the visions, principles, methods—and, yes, even the ocean of lyrics and melodies washing through the forest—that we were encountering in the mountains for real justice. Wild Goose was now less a "Peacepalooza" than an updated Highlander Center—the place in the neighboring state of Tennessee where, decades ago, many Civil Rights movement leaders got their training and some of their marching orders.

Rev. Barber invoked Dr. Martin Luther King, Jr. often. But to put it this way is not quite right. He wasn't so much speaking *about* Dr. King as he was speaking *to* and *with* Dr. King: as if he were here, as if he were with all of us in this forest. As if Rev. Barber were checking things with this great trans-historical mentor or ruminating on the state of things with him. There was something both intimate and revealing about this.

It was not surprising then that Rev. Barber closed on a Kingian note. He had detailed in his presentations the destruction the state was facing and the backlash that his movement was facing. Nevertheless, like Dr. King he was clear that he and the others organizing to stop this catastrophe were striving to love their enemies. "We must love our enemies," he said repeatedly, "so that we do not become what we hate."

In bringing these urgent dispatches from this emerging movement to the Wild Goose Festival, Rev. Barber was rolling both report and invitation into one powerful word, urging us to join this escalating campaign at the crossroads.

8

Alice Paul:
Pioneering Liberating Nonviolence

November 15, 2012

Turning points are easier to recognize long after they've occurred than while they're taking place. One of those shifts happened 100 years ago next month, setting in motion a dramatic strategy to achieve a goal first set 70 years before at the historic Seneca Falls Convention for women's equality: passing a constitutional amendment establishing the right of women to vote. Along the way this new direction would galvanize public opinion, provoke a brutal backlash from the government — including "the night of terror" that took place on November 15, 1917 — and prompt a transformation of political thinking that cleared the way for the passage of the 19th Amendment in 1920.

The appointment of Alice Paul as the Congressional Committee chair of the National American Woman Suffrage Association (NAWSA) at the organization's December 1912 convention in Philadelphia turned out to be this kind of catalyzing step. It revived a debate in the movement about how the goal of voting rights would be met — and it opened the door to the use of electrifying nonviolent action as a key to mobilizing the people power needed to dislodge an ancient plank of patriarchy. A century later we still have much to learn from this relentless agent for social change.

NAWSA, with its roots in the universal suffrage movement that began in the 1860s, focused on lobbying state governments as a path to voting rights. Paul, by contrast, believed — as did the earliest proponents of women's rights in the U.S., including Susan B. Anthony and Elizabeth Cady Stanton — that the surest route was passing an amendment to the U.S. Constitution. Immediately after becoming committee chairwoman, Paul pursued this direction by pouring her energy into organizing highly visible, public actions focused on the federal government, especially President Woodrow Wilson's administration.

Paul's organizing vision was rooted less in her academic accomplishments — just before taking her NAWSA post she finished her Ph.D. in economics at the University of Pennsylvania — than in the hands-on training she received from the premier women's suffrage organizers in Britain, including Emmeline and Christabel Pankhurst, whom she met and began collaborating with while studying social work. The Pankhursts' motto was "Deeds, not words." According to the Alice Paul Institute: "Believing that prayer, petitions, and patience was not enough to successfully enfranchise women, the Pankhursts engaged in direct and visible measures, such as heckling, window smashing, and rock throwing, to raise public awareness about the suffrage issue. Their notoriety gained them front-page coverage on many London newspapers, where they were seen being carried away in handcuffs by the police."

Paul, who joined in the Pankhurst actions and was jailed on several occasions, drew a key principle from this militancy: Actions must be undertaken that are visible, dramatic, capable of awakening the public and designed to empower women. When she returned to the U.S. in 1910, she said, "The militant policy is bringing success. ... The agitation has brought England out of her lethargy, and women of England are now talking of the time when they will vote, instead of the time when their children would vote, as was the custom a year or two back."

While not directly replicating in the U.S. the tactics of her British counterparts—there was no rock throwing or window-smashing in Paul's repertoire—she nonetheless was intent on recreating the dynamic they had achieved by organizing actions that brought maximum exposure to the issue.

In this vein she first organized the counter-inaugural Woman's Suffrage Parade of 1913 on March 3, the day before President Wilson's first inauguration. Five thousand women marched up Pennsylvania Avenue "in a spirit of protest against the present political organization of society, from which women are excluded," as the official program stated. The parade included 20 floats, nine marching bands, four mounted brigades and featured notables, including Helen Keller. It was led by lawyer Inez Millholland, who was riding a white horse. The marchers were harassed by "scores of male onlookers [who] attacked the suffragists, first with insults and obscenities, and then with physical violence, while the police stood by and watched."

This led to a Senate hearing, the replacement of the police superintendent and widespread national publicity.

The NAWSA had officially endorsed the parade but provided very little support, leaving Paul to do most of the work of organizing volunteers and raising funds. This signaled the underlying divergence in strategies, which eventually led to Paul breaking with the NAWSA and founding the National Women's Party (NWP). After Wilson won re-election, the NWP organized the "Silent Sentinels," which were groups of women who picketed daily in front of the White House, beginning in January 1917.

At first, Wilson ignored the group, but this changed after the United States entered World War I in April. Picketers — whose signs stressed the contradiction of Wilson's "war for democracy" when half the U.S. population couldn't vote — began to be arrested on a charge of "obstructing traffic" and were jailed when they refused to pay fines. They were also assaulted verbally and physically by members of the public, with the police doing nothing to protect them. Through most of 1917, women were arrested in front of the White House, and many chose jail over paying fines. Despite objections from some in Congress, in September a committee was created in the House of Representatives to deal with the issue of women's suffrage.

On October 20 Paul was arrested and sentenced to seven months in prison. She, like many of the other women, was sent to the Occoquan Workhouse, where she was placed in solitary confinement with nothing to eat but bread and water. When she grew weak she was dispatched to the prison hospital, where she began a hunger strike that other women joined. She was remanded to a psychiatric ward and threatened with being sent to an insane asylum. She was force-fed and subjected to systematic sleep deprivation.

Then, on the night of November 15, numerous suffragists held at the Occoquan Workhouse were brutalized. As Louise Bernikow reports, 33 suffragists were beaten and kicked by club-wielding guards. News of the attack was carried by the press, and a court-ordered hearing two weeks later determined that they had been terrorized simply for exercising their right to protest. Eventually they were all released.

In January 1918, Wilson dramatically shifted position by throwing his support behind women's suffrage and urging Congress to pass the amendment. (Intriguingly, he framed this as an urgently needed "war measure.") The House rapidly passed it, but the Senate didn't take it up until October, where it failed by two votes. The NWP and other organizations maintained the picketing regimen at the White House, resulting in another wave of arrests and jailings. They campaigned in the off-year election against anti-suffrage candidates, which helped ensure that most members of Congress were pro-suffrage. By June 4, 1919, the Senate and House of Representatives had passed the amendment, and by August the following year the required 36 states had ratified it.

In the last half-century, numerous nonviolent campaigns and movements have taken up the tactics that Alice Paul pioneered, and yet we still have much to marvel at and learn from.

Rather than being defeated by the imprisonment, harassment, beatings, torture and force-feeding, this movement responded to this institutionalized viciousness with stubbornly nonviolent resolve. It threw into sharp relief the systemic violence of male privilege as well as the particular forms of violence it uses to protect that privilege. In a time when we face systemic injustice of all types — including systemic gender violence — this kind of strategic resolve is needed now more than ever.

But this movement wasn't only determined — it was in for the long haul. The NWP and other groups sustained their picket in front of the White House for *two and a half years.* Historian Linda G. Ford estimates that between 1917 and 1919 approximately 2,000 women took part in the picket and that 500 women were arrested, with 168 serving time in jail.

The women's suffrage movement reaches out to us from across the intervening century with a powerful example of longevity, discipline and strategic purpose. As we stand at another turning point — in a very different time, but facing many of the structures that made that movement 100 years ago necessary — this rich history urges us forward to also engage the monumental challenges of the 21st century with a similar gutsy persistence, laser-like purpose and willingness to assume risk.

9

Carol Bragg: Fasting for a Revolution in Values

January 5, 2013

The December 14, 2011 rampage that claimed the lives of 28 people, including 20 children, in Newtown, Conn., has prompted a vigorous new debate on gun violence in the United States and the emergence of a spate of legislative proposals that the president and Congress may broach sometime this year. While policies designed to outlaw or control guns are needed now more than ever, for many of us these efforts must be rooted in a larger imperative: coming to grips with the culture of violence that makes this kind of tragedy possible and seeing our way clear to an alternative.

It is this deeper prompting that compelled Carol Bragg to begin a 30-day fast on January 1 calling on the nation's political leadership "to embrace the revolution in values and commitment to nonviolence that are part of the legacy of Dr. Martin Luther King, Jr."

A former staff person for the American Friends Service Committee who served on the National Council of the Fellowship of Reconciliation, Bragg's appeal calls for a National Day of Prayer and Reflection on individual and collective responsibility for violence, the appointment of a multidisciplinary National Advisory Commission on the Causes of Violence in America, the incorporation of nonviolence education into elementary and secondary school curricula, study by the academic community of the history and causes of violence, and a commitment by faith communities to teach their members and the larger world how to love unconditionally. She is also hoping to prompt a meeting between President Obama and civil rights movement veterans to discuss concrete ways these dimensions of a "revolution in values and commitment to nonviolence" can be promoted and applied.

Bragg's resolve to launch this fast was deepened by her work over the past year as part of a team digitizing Dr. Martin Luther King, Jr.'s sermons, speeches, articles, interviews and press statements for the King Center website. This immersion in the thought and vision of Dr. King convinced her "that the only thing that can prevent this country from spiraling down the path to self-destruction is a great spiritual revolution accompanied by experimentation with nonviolence in every aspect of life and at every level of human existence — from our urban streets and rural roads to our state houses to the halls of Congress, to the international level."

While catalyzed by the violence at Newtown, Bragg's action intends to highlight the numerous historic milestones in the history of nonviolent change that will be marked this year, including the 50th anniversary of the civil rights movement's Birmingham campaign, its monumental March on Washington and, on the first day of her fast this past Tuesday, the 150th anniversary of the Emancipation Proclamation on January 1.

Bragg is no stranger to fasting. In 1974 she undertook a 62-day fast at the U.S. Capitol calling for an end to U.S. funding for the war in Vietnam. As she reports, this fast began as a personal witness but then expanded into a 17-organization project. In 1988 she fasted for 19 days in support of stronger U.S. sanctions against South Africa's apartheid regime.

Fasting has a time-honored place in a wide range of religious traditions for ritualistic, mystical, ascetic, or other spiritual or ethical purposes. At the same time, it is also a venerable tactic of nonviolent change. In ancient Ireland, for example, it was a recognized method for dealing with injustice: "The ancient Irish law books, of which several survive, explain that a person could fast against a man who had injured him in some way and who was of a higher social rank. The wronged individual went to the wrongdoer's house and sat outside from dawn to dusk refusing to eat. By so doing he brought bad luck or 'pollution' to his

47

opponent. The one fasted against then had two options. He could either admit his wrong and redress it — the fasting would stop and social harmony would be restored. Or he could counter fast to ward off the curse."

The power of this Irish practice — which apparently has parallels in India — seems rooted in the energy that flows, not from violent confrontation, but from conscious nonviolent restraint and by dramatizing in one's own flesh the injustice at hand. Instead of unleashing counter-violence that reinforces the opponent's defensiveness, the faster engages in a culturally permissible ritual that opens psychological space but also likely created compelling, nonviolent pressure for a just resolution.

Gandhi fasted "for the unfoldment of the spirit" and in solidarity with the poor, but also for social transformation, including stopping communal riots in India. Fasting was a regular feature of his activism and many since then, including César Chávez, who fasted to help the United Farm Workers maintain nonviolent discipline. Fasting has been a regular feature of many movements and campaigns.

In my own life, some of the most powerful nonviolent actions I have witnessed have included long fasts for peace and justice, including the 1983 Fast for Life for Nuclear Disarmament and the 1986 Veterans' Fast for Life on the steps of the U.S. Capitol calling for an end to the United States' wars in Central America. My co-worker Friar Louie Vitale has engaged in numerous long fasts. I joined him once for a 21-day fast working to dismantle anti-homeless laws in San Francisco in 1995.

The most compelling faster in my experience was Rev. David Duncombe, a long-time campus minister at the medical school at the University of California at San Francisco. After his friend Brian Willson was run down by a munitions train at Concord Naval Weapons Station in Northern California in 1987, Duncombe was arrested once a week for six years blocking trains and trucks transporting military weapons headed to Central

America. During one of his stints in jail he did a 40-day fast. Later, he drew on this experience when he turned his attention to international debt relief. He joined the campaign to forgive the sweltering debt that was crushing poor nations and their citizens around the globe. From 2000 to 2007, he fasted three times for at least 40 days, each time at the U.S. Capitol. He spent each day visiting Congressional offices. As he lost weight and energy, he sought to quietly demonstrate what hunger looks like. When one of the debt relief bills was about to come up for a vote, a conservative senator sent him a hand-written note saying he would be voting for it because of Duncombe's witness.

There is no guarantee that fasting will have this kind of impact. Carol Bragg knows this. But she has also experienced its quiet power. When she fasted to protest apartheid in 1988, she sought to influence Senator Claiborne Pell of Rhode Island, who then was the chair of the Senate Foreign Relations Committee. Pell opposed sanctions on philosophical grounds. "I had to assure him," Bragg now recalls, "that I would never ask him to vote against his conscience but was fasting only to express the depth of my convictions on this subject. Six weeks later, when the hearing was held, he announced his reluctant support. During a recess in the hearing, he made his way to the back of the hearing room to shake my hand and tell me he was reading a biography of Gandhi. This was my best use of soul-force."

Each of us can experiment with this transformational power. Bragg is doing this, at the moment, with the loving but determined method of fasting, inspired anew by the vision and action of Dr. King. Her fast calls on all of us to reflect, act and build a world where this compelling cooperative power is unleashed to quench the fires of violence and injustice.

10

Sandra Steingraber:
The Scientist's Experiment

April 25, 2013

Sandra Steingraber, the renowned biologist, author, poet and cancer survivor, is serving a 15-day sentence for interfering with the smooth, forward motion of the burgeoning fracking industry. In March, Ithaca College's Distinguished Scholar in Residence in Environmental Studies and Science joined the Seneca Lake 12 in blocking the driveway of Inergy Midstream, an energy storage and transportation company in upstate New York that plans to pump highly pressurized gas derived from far-off fracking fields into salt caverns along and under a lake which provides drinking water for 100,000 people in the area. She and two others — Melissa Chipman and Michael Dineen — were sentenced to jail time after refusing to pay $375 fines.

For a quarter century Dr. Steingraber has ceaselessly researched, documented, written about and worked against the hazards of industrial impacts on the planet and its inhabitants. Integrating powerful prose with scientific findings, her pivotal books include *Living Downstream: An Ecologist Looks at Cancer and the Environment* (1997), *Having Faith: An Ecologist's Journey to Motherhood* (2001), and *Raising Elijah: Protecting Our Children in an Age of Environmental Crisis* (2011). At the same time, she has been active in New York's campaign to prevent fracking in the state.

Her sentence in the Chemung County Jail in Elmira, N.Y., which began on April 17 — just hours after being interviewed by Bill Moyers on his public affairs program — hasn't seemed to slow her down. Before going in, she told 350.org's Bill McKibben that she planned to use her time to carry on with writing projects and a list of other tasks.

A part of this work-plan, presumably, was the letter that ran on *Common Dreams* on Earth Day that she had written in her cell "with a borrowed pencil on the back of the 'Chemung County Inmate Request Form,' which is a half sheet of paper." (This scarcity of writing materials calls to mind Dr. Martin Luther King, Jr. scratching out the "Letter from a Birmingham Jail" on toilet paper and along the margins of a handy newspaper half a century ago.) In addition to commenting on the jail's surreal arbitrariness, rote institutional heartlessness, and even a small act of inmate resistance followed by an unexpected victory — all on display in the first couple of days inside — Steingraber shares three reasons she's chosen to go to jail.

First, to resist the industrialization of the Finger Lakes region that will "aid and abet the fracking industry by erecting a massive storage depot near the birthplace of my son."

Second, to respond to a recent commentary by economist Jeremy Grantham published in the journal *Nature*. Real-life data is overtaking even the worst-case scenarios for climate change, Grantham wrote, therefore scientists must take action. "Be persuasive, be bold, be arrested (if necessary)," he urged. Steingraber decided to answer this call.

Third, to signal her commitment to resisting the mounting extinction of species. This pledge was rooted in an experience she had had several years ago when her son had asked her to make him a polar bear costume for Halloween and, as she was doing so, she became acutely aware that this outfit would likely outlive the species itself. "Out on the street that night I saw many species heading towards extinction; children dressed as frogs, bees, monarch butterflies, and the icon of Halloween itself — the little brown bat. The kinship that children feel for animals and their ongoing disappearance from us literally brought me to my knees that night, on a sidewalk in my own village. It was love that got me back up. It was love that brought me to this jail cell," Steingraber wrote.

51

Her letter stresses the indissoluble link between the personal and the political. Steingraber's writing typically brings the wealth of scientific data into focus with the particularity of lives directly impacted by massive economic, political and environmental forces of industrialized society. It began with her own experience of bladder cancer in her 20s (with indications that it was related to an apparent cancer cluster in her hometown and within her family) and has been an enduring focus of much of her research in one way or another. It also comes through in the poignancy of her book titles, striking a chord both deeply personal and almost uniformly applicable to people everywhere.

Real lives and real bodies are impacted by the regime of toxics within which we subsist — a fact that sharpens the meaning and power of Steingraber's act of civil disobedience, which is nothing if not embodied resistance. Nonviolent change ultimately hinges on launching and sustaining a powerful, searching and inclusive conversation across society in order to wrestle with the problems before us and to achieve effective solutions. Often this means a long-term process of a society changing its mind. If we have been taught nothing else over the past century since Gandhi illuminated the potential for nonviolent social transformation, the most powerful language at our disposal for this conversation are our vulnerable, unarmed, resilient and grounded bodies. It is not enough to enunciate our opposition or write out our positions. We must put our entire selves forward.

In the face of the monumental risks to the body of the world (and all the bodies that huddle across it) posed by the toxic tsunami we face, Steingraber and others are putting their own bodies a bit at risk by standing in the way of the catastrophe's seeming inevitability. By doing so, they begin to counter what Steingraber has called "informed futility syndrome" — the way greater knowledge about a problem actually can incapacitate us. The more we know, the more paralyzed we often become. Taking action, placing our bodies in the nonviolent fray, has a way of thawing out our frozen immobility.

Another theme of Gandhi's seems to be operating here. He called his autobiography, *My Experiments with Truth*, which largely consisted of stories about his experimentation with nonviolence in his own life and in the larger world. Using a basic version of the scientific method, he learned by doing, and invited his readers to do the same. *Don't take my word for the power of nonviolent resistance,* he seemed to say. *Go out and experiment with this yourself.* Scientist Sandra Steingraber has been conducting a long-term experiment on the viability and sustainability of the planet and the well-being of its inhabitants. *Can we sound the alarm? Can we change direction? What will it take?* Now the mounting data has led her to her next experiment — going to jail — because she does not want only to explain the world but to change it.

By doing so, she stands in a long line of scientists who are led not simply to analyze but to translate their findings into action, like the Manhattan Project scientists who turned away in horror at what they created in the New Mexico desert and formed the basis of the enduring anti-nuclear weapons movement; or Carl Sagan, who was led by his grasp of the beauty of the universe to warn us of nuclear winter and to be arrested at the Nevada Test Site engaging in nonviolent civil disobedience in 1987; or James Hansen, the former head of NASA's Goddard Institute for Space Studies who has "spoken truth to power" about climate change, and has faced the consequences for doing so.

Scientists conduct experiments to increase humanity's knowledge and to establish practical applications. If we think of Sandra Steingraber's act of civil disobedience not simply as a political witness but as a scientific experiment, it will meet its objective only, like all experiments, when its outcomes can be verified over and over again. In this case, it would mean replicating outcomes like freeing us from our debilitating incapacity for change, deepening and broadening a movement for a sustainable world, or actually seeing this world starting to come into being.

Dr. Sandra Steinberger is behind bars. If we want to honor her witness, we can take up the experiment she's been working on and replicate it in our own way. Inspired by Steingraber and a growing international movement, we have an opportunity to conduct our own nonviolent experiment with truth for a more sustainable world.

11

Carol Parks-Haun and Ron Walters: The Wichita Sit-Ins

July 19, 2012

The 1960 lunch-counter sit-ins in Greensboro, North Carolina hold an honored place in U.S. history. This campaign had an impact far beyond the concrete success it achieved in ending the policy of racial segregation in Woolworth's department stores across the southern United States. It made national headlines that sparked similar sit-ins for racial desegregation in 54 cities in nine states throughout the South and catalyzed the next phase of the civil rights movement by inspiring the formation of the Student Nonviolent Coordinating Committee.

The Greensboro sit-ins, though, were not the first ones. Earlier sit-ins (sometimes called sit-downs, recalling the labor movement's strikes in the 1930s) were organized in Chicago (1942), St. Louis (1949) and Baltimore (1952). There was even a sit-in at a then-segregated public library in Alexandria, Virginia, in 1939. Many of these were part of larger campaigns, like the Chicago actions organized by the Congress of Racial Equality and fueled by studying Krishnalal Shridharani's *War Without Violence,* a book outlining Gandhi's method for nonviolent change published a few years earlier.

But not all sit-ins were part of strategic campaigns supported by large organizations. Two years before Greensboro, a handful of students in Wichita, Kansas — including Carol Parks-Haun and her cousin Ron Walters — decided to challenge the discriminatory policies of the downtown Dockum Drug Store where, like many other establishments throughout the city and across the South, African-Americans were prevented from sitting at its lunch counters.

Though Parks-Haun and Walters were active members of the local chapter of the National Association for the Advancement of Colored People, the organization did not officially throw its weight behind this effort, since the NAACP typically shunned direct action strategies. Nonetheless, inspired by the Little Rock Nine and the Montgomery Bus Boycott, the students were determined to take action.

As they cast around for a way forward, they heard about a sit-in by students at a California college "who ended segregation at a campus restaurant by occupying it with students reading newspapers all day long." This was the spark they needed. They decided to see if they, too, could begin the process of dismantling Jim Crow in their own hometown. Years later they would speak of the inner challenges they faced, knowing that their action, however peaceful, might provoke a violent, racist backlash, and how they prepared themselves by undergoing challenging role-plays in a local church basement.

On July 19, 1958 ten students of color filtered into the drug store and were denied service. The Kansas Historical Society summarizes what turned out to be a three-week effort:

> The students continued to fill the drug store. A few white patrons cursed at them and questioned them, but the students held strong. Only a couple of times were they threatened. [The police ran them off once.] Finally on August 11 the owner relented, saying, "Serve them — I'm losing too much money." This victory for the students became a victory for equality in Kansas. With one downtown store no longer practicing segregation, other retail establishments slowly began to change their policies in Wichita and throughout Kansas. On August 19 NAACP Youth Council students in Oklahoma City, who had been in contact with Walters, began their own sit-in.

All of the Dockum stores in Kansas were eventually desegregated, while the successful sit-in at Oklahoma City's Katz Drug Store helped spread this tactic. Despite these consequences, though, the story of the Dockum sit-ins went largely unnoticed.

When the Dockum Drug Store sit-in first happened in July 1958, few heard about it or recognized its importance. The sit-in was a student-led effort to end segregation. The two local daily newspapers published little about it, avoiding the negative association with the protest. The local chapter of the National Association for the Advancement of Colored People gave moral support, but did not participate in the student effort.

By all accounts, this story was chiefly remembered for decades only by the participants, even though it set "a precedent that really began what would be a very significant strategy — a strategy that would change the way business was done in the United States," according to Wichita historian and author Gretchen Eick. In the past decade or so, this historical turning point has been increasingly recognized, with the production of a documentary and video report, a story on NPR ("Kansas Sit-In Gets Its Due at Last") and the creation of a 20-foot-long bronze sculpture in downtown Wichita with a lunch counter and patrons engaging in this successful protest.

In spite of this gradual recovery of the memory of this sit-in, its relative disappearance over decades raises many tantalizing questions about our collective memory. Why are some acts of nonviolent resistance remembered and why are others less so?

In this case there were concrete factors. There was the lack of the organizational support that typically not only helps to build actions but also to magnify them, to spread them, to saturate the social circles of others who care. There was the seemingly deliberate lack of media attention — the NPR story stresses that this campaign "failed to achieve national visibility in large part because the local newspaper didn't want to scare away advertisers." But there also seems to be a kind of capriciousness, some things simply capture people's attention, while other things don't "take." Was this seemingly arbitrary quality itself due to a certain lack of drama, because the opponents gave in quickly? Was there less at stake for the power-holders in Kansas than, say, Tennessee or Mississippi? Was the story less compelling because there was a quiet undertow to the whole thing?

While all of these factors may have been at play, there is also the mysterious growth of movements. The courageous action in Wichita helped nourish a coming wave of change. It helped lay the groundwork for this power. It helped explore possibilities and tap potentialities. As a subscriber to Bill Moyer's Eight Stages of a Social Movement outlines in his book *Doing Democracy*, I wonder whether the Wichita sit-ins may have been part of those first three foundational stages where, for most of the populace, the movement does not yet exist, but such prefigurative actions are testing the waters, creating openings, experimenting with new ways, even when they stand in consternating contrast to old ways—including, for example, those tried and true methods of the NAACP. Without those foundations, the Take Off Stage — the full rocketing power of Greensboro — is likely not possible.

The lesson? At whatever stage, action is important, even if it takes decades or longer to glimpse its magnificent and generative power.

12
Narayan Desai:
A Gandhian in Birmingham
March 29, 2012

As I flew in from Illinois, the thunderstorms over Birmingham cleared long enough to let us land in good order. I had come to Alabama to attend a retreat featuring Narayan Desai, one of the last living disciples of Mohandas Gandhi, who made the trip there from India at the invitation of longtime activists and authors Shelley and Jim Douglass. Born in 1924 in Gandhi's ashram, Desai has consistently undertaken Gandhian work for eight decades, and has recently published a 2,300-page biography of Gandhi. It was not only deeply moving to spend three days last week in the presence of this life-long Gandhian, but to do so in Birmingham, the site of one of the civil rights movement's most iconic struggles.

Even as several friends and I were collected at the airport and driven to the retreat center, I was vividly aware with each passing mile that we were traversing holy ground. This terrain resounds with a process for freedom set in motion a half century ago: a decision by African-American children, women and men to join together in concerted and bold nonviolent resistance for full and equal participation in society.

I believe that places where human beings band together for transformative justice become sites of enduring power. I first felt this in the 1990s when I was part of a bicultural team leading nonviolence retreats with Latino/a youths in California's Central Valley. The land itself seemed imbued with the determination, courage and creativity of the migrant poor who, against very long odds, built the United Farm Workers and engaged in protracted — but ultimately successful — strikes and campaigns that sought the right to organize, increased wages and improved working conditions.

Such an inheritance can reframe how we see such land: from a terrain of oppression to a topography of liberation. This alternative overlay doesn't erase the facts of injustice. Rather, it retrieves and holds dear the creative and stubborn ways injustice has been challenged through time. I suspect that virtually every acre on earth has not only been subject to domination and injustice, but also to struggles for justice. One of our jobs as agents of change is to rescue the memory of this seen and unseen resistance.

Birmingham has done this through the magnificent Birmingham Civil Rights Institute, which captures the history of oppression that the self-styled Magic City lived for decades, as well as the intricate details of a movement for nonviolent change that rose up to challenge it. The museum is situated directly across the street from the 16th Avenue Baptist Church, where four little girls — Addie Mae Collins, Denise McNair, Carole Robertson and Cynthia Wesley — died when the church was bombed on September 15, 1963. During the pivotal Birmingham campaign that took place earlier that year, thousands of young people gathered in that same church and headed out to make history. In watching films over the years from that momentous protest, I had somehow thought that they had processed quite a way before meeting the police. I was wrong; directly across the street is Kelly Ingram Park, where a storm of water cannons and German shepherds was turned on the youth of the city. The park is now studded with sculptures and statues memorializing the turning point that in many ways helped re-map Birmingham and the nation.

Gandhi's Indian independence movement was also about re-mapping: transforming a terrain of colonial conquest to a nation under self-rule. Over the weekend, Narayan Desai shared his experience of this geographical and spiritual re-inscription. The three gifts of Gandhi that Desai illuminated were ashram observances (the vows and principles that Gandhi developed and served as the source for action, by which one can "convert personal virtues into social values"), the constructive program (18 comprehensive social programs), and Satyagraha (soul-force, truth-force and love-force activated for nonviolent social change). In both constructing new institutions and organizing many large and small Satyagraha campaigns — including the 240-mile Salt March in 1930 — the Gandhian movement was slowly reframing how one saw and understood India.

As we know, the power of this re-mapping went far beyond the subcontinent. In the U.S., Gandhi's vision and practice inspired numerous key figures in the civil rights movement, including Howard Thurman, Bayard Rustin and James Lawson. A few years after the Montgomery Bus Boycott, where Gandhi's ideas had been seminal, Martin Luther King Jr. journeyed to India to immerse himself even more fully in Gandhi's vision of soul-force. Gandhi's grandson Arun Gandhi tells the story that, during this trip, King visited a museum which had previously been a private home where Gandhi often stayed. During the tour, King became fascinated with the sparse room where Gandhi slept and abruptly announced that he would be spending the night there. The museum official showing him around was bewildered and resistant. No one was allowed to stay in this room, he told his guest; besides, there were no amenities for him here. But King insisted and, after the official made a call to his superiors in the Indian government, he prevailed.

Apparently, King was eager to make contact with the spirit of Gandhi as he prepared for the next phase of his work. Just before leaving India, Dr. King was interviewed on national radio, and he said:

> Since being in India, I am more convinced than ever before that the method of non-violent resistance is the most potent weapon available to oppressed people in their

struggle for justice and human dignity. In a real sense, Mahatma Gandhi embodied in his life certain universal principles that are inherent in the moral structure of the universe, and these principles are as inescapable as the law of gravitation.

Just as King seized the opportunity to grow closer to Gandhi during his Indian pilgrimage, those of us who were in Birmingham last week had a chance to grow a bit closer to him through Narayan Desai, as we prepare for the next phase of our work for a nonviolent world.

For decades, Desai has carried on Gandhi's mission in many ways — such as collecting three million acres of land for the poor as part of Vinobe Bhave's Land Gift movement, and organizing Gandhi's Shanti Sena or "Peace Army" along the northern border when there were tensions with China — but, after being in his presence for a few days, it seemed to me that he has done this most profoundly by, over many decades, imbibing and sharing Gandhi's spirit.

Narayan Desai died on March 15, 2015 in Surat, India.

13

Wangari Maathai: Connecting the Dots

September 29, 2011

The first thing Wangari Maathai did after being notified that she had won the 2004 Nobel Peace Prize was to plant a tree in her backyard. She said she did this whenever she celebrated something.

Maathai recently died of ovarian cancer in Nairobi. This is a time for mourning but also for celebration of a life lived full on: challenging poverty, empowering women, resisting exploitation, cultivating democracy, and advocating for the integrity and sustainability of the planet.

She tied all these dimensions of her life together through both the simplicity and complexity of planting trees. Since 1977 her Green Belt Movement planted 40 million of them throughout Africa.

Tree planting was simple because it was designed to be something women could do with their two hands close to home, including harvesting native seeds in their area.

At the same time tree planting was complex because it became a way of linking human rights, poverty, environmental protection, justice and peace.

When Gandhi sought a symbolic but also dramatically hands-on practice to signify and center the Indian independence movement, he reached for the spinning wheel. This everyday implement was charged by Gandhi with the power of resisting imperialist oppression (spinning one's own cloth in defiance of a colonial system by which Indian raw materials were transported to English factories and then sold back at markup to the Indian market) and portending a new political and economic future.

Planting trees was Maathai's spinning wheel. It directly challenged a system of desertification in Kenya and throughout the continent that had left millions of ordinary people destitute and without resources. In her Nobel Prize acceptance speech she shared how her own activism was rooted in childhood memories of rural Kenya, where she had experienced forests being cleared for commercial agriculture, destroying biodiversity and the capacity of forests to conserve water.

"There is no word in our language for 'desert,'" Maathai once said. The desertification of her country was a relatively recent consequence of modernity and globalization, and she was inspired to change this.

At the same time, as the tangled threads of land use, markets, and dictatorial policies became clear, she was also committed to undoing another desert: the lack of a thriving and democratic civil society. "The tree," Maathai said, "became a symbol for the democratic struggle in Kenya. Citizens were mobilized to challenge widespread abuses of power, corruption and environmental mismanagement."

Organizing widespread tree planting defied the vested interests profiting from vast resource exploitation and the national government that supported them, including the 24-year dictatorship of President Daniel Arap Moi.

Maathai's basic practice of environmental conservation and local sustainability—tree planting throughout the country—became a potent ritual that challenged the political and economic structures of power.

Just how potent this movement was can be measured by the fierce attacks Maathai faced over and over again.

Maathai was vilified, beaten and arrested many times as she and her colleagues organized numerous campaigns to stop the privatization of large sections of the Karuna Forest outside Nairobi (in which Maathai and her cohorts were physically attacked by 200 hired thugs as she planted trees) and the destruction of a large park in Nairobi slated for a huge office complex. In both cases, the campaigns were successful.

In 1992 Maathai discovered that her name was on a government assassination list; she barricaded herself in her home for three days before government soldiers broke in and arrested her. Following an international outcry, she was released. Later that year she and others engaged in a hunger strike in a city park to pressure the government to release a group of political prisoners. The police forcibly removed the fasters, during which Maathai was clubbed and hospitalized. Again, international supporters rallied on her behalf. Eventually the political prisoners were released.

Wangari Maathai was an epochal figure who, in her vision, strategic organizing, and the willingness inexorably to deliver her message in person and to face the risks of doing so, spelled out the possibility of responding to the unique challenges facing our planet and its inhabitants in our time. Just as Gandhi heralded the age of decolonization, Maathai dramatically signaled the emergence of the age of global indigenous eco-justice.

There are other resonances with Gandhi. Maathai, like Gandhi, saw the particular problem in front of her as part of a system of injustice that demanded a holistic response. Maathai, like Gandhi, relentlessly gambled that nonviolent people power was capable of shaking and even dismantling structures of oppression. In so doing, Maathai challenged deeply entrenched interests, empowered women as agents of change, and inspired the global environmental movement. Like the forest itself, her work provided canopy for many species of transformative initiatives, including civic and environmental education, capacity building and income generation, and programs nurturing food security, human rights and self-determination.

Finally, like Gandhi, Maathai articulated the link between her work and a practical vision of peace:

> It is evident that many wars are fought over resources which are now becoming increasingly scarce. If we

conserved our resources better, fighting over them would not then occur. ... So, protecting the global environment is directly related to securing peace. ... Those of us who understand the complex concept of the environment have the burden to act. We must not tire, we must not give up, we must persist.

Wangari Maathai is our great teacher from whom we will continue to learn for a very long time. We celebrate her life, work, legacy, and power. And like her, we can do so by planting a tree—or by engaging in an appropriate equivalent.

Whatever we do, let us, like Wangari Maathai, recognize the power we have to revive and replenish this fragile and resilient world.

14
José Ramos-Horta:
East Timor and the Nonviolent Option
August 30, 2012

On August 30, 1999 the people of East Timor took to the polls in
a United Nations-sponsored referendum on the future of their
country, with over 80 percent of this small Pacific nation voting
for independence from Indonesia. In the run up to the vote,
observers had witnessed shootings, beatings and a climate of
intimidation aimed at pro-independence Timorese and fomented
by paramilitaries supported by the Indonesian military. After the
overwhelming vote favoring freedom, the Indonesian violence
dramatically escalated. Many East Timorese were killed, with as
many as 500,000 displaced. This calamitous destruction
galvanized international outrage, and within a few weeks a U.N.-
mandated International Force for East Timor was deployed, with
the task of restoring peace and overseeing the country's transition
to independence. East Timor became an internationally
recognized, independent nation on May 20, 2002.

Controlled by the Portuguese since the 16th century and rich
in timber and offshore natural gas, East Timor had been
decolonized in 1975, only to be promptly invaded and occupied
by Indonesia in a military operation green-lighted by U.S.
President Gerald Ford and his Secretary of State, Henry Kissinger.
A brutal counter-insurgency campaign was waged for decades
against the armed resistance that sprang up after the invasion.
Though U.N. resolutions condemned Indonesia's land grab and
the massive violence that ensued, Western governments did
nothing to challenge this arrangement.

In the late 1980s, the resistance set a new course, largely
shifting from armed struggle — which had proved ineffective in

dislodging Indonesia's withering domination — to a strategy focused on nonviolent campaigns inside East Timor, in Indonesia and internationally. As Erica Chenoweth and Maria Stephan report:

> The first major protest occurred in November 1988, when Pope John Paul II was invited by [Indonesian] President Suharto to [East Timor's capital] Dili, an act meant to bestow further legitimacy on the forced annexation. During the pope's mass, which was attended by thousands, a group of East Timorese youths ran up to the altar and began shouting pro-independence slogans and unfurled banners calling on Indonesian forces to leave. The demonstration, covered by the media, embarrassed Indonesia, showed the face of East Timorese opposition to the outside world, and helped lower the levels of fear among the East Timorese.

Three years later, the Indonesian military opened fire on a pro-independence procession to the Santa Cruz cemetery in Dili, killing 271 participants. Unlike past atrocities, this one was filmed and photographed by Western journalists. Amy Goodman and Alain Nairn, who were badly beaten during the military attack, managed to get the story out. This event helped spark the emergence of an international solidarity movement, including the founding of the East Timor Action Network.

In 1994 my friend and colleague Rev. John Chamberlin visited East Timor and made an irrevocable commitment to work for its freedom. A United Methodist minister based in San Francisco, California, Chamberlin created East Timor Religious Outreach, and cajoled a handful of us to help organize a series of marches and nonviolent civil disobedience actions at the Indonesian consulate beginning in 1994 and carrying on through the 1990s. These were small but heartfelt protests, vigils and prayer services held at the consulate's modern building a stone's throw from Fisherman's Wharf. Our actions drew a lot of notice from the streams of tourists headed up Columbus Avenue toward North Beach, especially when a few of us would scale the gate and, ensconced in the doorway, proceed with our speeches until we were handcuffed and led away by the police. Eventually, we were invited to join the National Council of Churches East Timor Task Force, where we helped develop an organizing plan for alerting and mobilizing religious communities to the Timorese struggle. This included staging a national strategy retreat for religious leadership, organizing delegations of clergy to visit East Timor, and attempting to build momentum for a shift in U.S. policy.

Most of the time, though, it felt like no progress was being made. And we in the U.S. were not the only ones who felt this. At one point José Ramos-Horta (the de facto East Timorese ambassador who traveled the world pleading his country's case and seeking international support) came to town and, in a meeting he had with a couple of us, shared his personal sense that things had bogged down. He couldn't see a way forward. He would continue the work, but nothing seemed to be breaking. We got to talking about a model that I had found helpful in organizing — Bill Moyer's "Eight Stages of a Successful Social Movement" — but the thickness of the fog was impervious to models, even those that might hint at a hidden momentum feeding on all that had taken place since the beginning of the struggle.

There comes a point when you enter a nowhere land, where the future is utterly unclear. In spite of this impenetrable mystery, though, you carry on — which is what Ramos-Horta and many others did.

Then, unexpectedly, the skies began to clear.

Ramos-Horta and Catholic Bishop Carlos Filipe Ximenes Belo were awarded the Nobel Peace Prize in 1996, drawing new international attention to the conflict. Next, a largely nonviolent pro-democracy movement brought regime change in Indonesia in

1998. The internal and international pressures for a shift by Indonesia on East Timor accelerated, which led to the 1999 referendum.

Ken Preston, my colleague at Pace e Bene Nonviolence Service, served on a United Nations-certified delegation to observe the referendum. As soon as he returned to the U.S. we held a press conference in front of the Indonesian consulate, where he recounted the widespread human rights violations he had witnessed. In contrast with this violence, though, Preston detailed the nonviolence of the Timorese people, including the decision by the resistance not to deploy the remaining armed fighters that were stationed in the hills. As Chenoweth and Stephan spell out:

> During this post-referendum violence, [long-time Timorese leader Kay Xanana] Gusmão called on the FALANTIL guerrillas to remain inside their cantonments and not to resist with military force. Gusmão later defended this decision, saying, "We did not want to be drawn into their game and their orchestration of violence in a civil war... We never expected such a dimension in the rampage that followed." On September 14, 2000, the UN Security Council voted unanimously to authorize an Australian-led international force for East Timor.

As Ramos-Horta has recently underscored in an essay directed at the Syrian opposition, the Timorese resistance opted for nonviolent methods for strategic — but also moral — reasons, and thereby, as another commentator puts it, "transformed the violence of the occupation into a weapon against the opposition."

There is no end to the challenges of independence, including the monumental problems of poverty, political divisions, injustice, and violence, which Ramos-Horta (who has served as East Timor's prime minister and president) experienced directly when he survived an assassination attempt in 2008. As we are learning, successful nonviolent people-power movements that end dictatorships and occupations do not automatically create thriving societies. Nonviolent change is messy. Hence the need for persistence and its role in dispelling the fog. Ramos-Horta has practiced this kind of persistence, and so have people like John Chamberlin, who has been back to East Timor almost every year since his first trip in the early 1990s. Though he will be retiring officially from the ministry next year, he tells me that his work for East Timor will go on and on.

We are living in a special time that is disclosing many lessons concerning the power, techniques and gumption that people-power movements for monumental change require, from the Filipino movement that toppled Marcos to the Arab Spring that brought down dictatorships in Tunisia and Egypt. There are many keys to the effectiveness of this nonviolent option, including a stubborn relentlessness even when the feedback loop runs dry. East Timor is yet another case of this persistent and harrowing journey that, like all the others, offers us clues for taking action as we move forward into the unknown future of nonviolent transformation.

15

Thomas Merton and Teju Cole:
Seven Short Stories for Our Times
January 31, 2013

Today is Thomas Merton's birthday. The American monk and prolific author died in 1968, but for some of us his spirit lingers, if only because the discoveries he was making in the last decade of his life still have traction. In the 1960s Merton found himself methodically dissolving the walls that his religious life had stringently erected between himself and the world. With growing clarity, he realized that his job as a monk was to breach these barriers and to enter deeply into the planet's woundedness and sacredness — which for him meant speaking up relentlessly for peace and nonviolence. Even when his superiors silenced him he kept at it, circulating letters and articles on war and peace through an informal network of friends and colleagues. Eventually the order lifted its ban and an unshackled Merton published a steady stream of essays and books on what he took to be the great spiritual crisis of his age.

Through his writings and occasional face-to-face encounters, Merton increasingly became a mentor and spiritual advisor for peace and justice activists. Part of what drew these change agents to a monk stationed in the knobby hills of Kentucky was his ability to connect the dots, for example, between the nuclear arms race and its spiritual foundations, as he demonstrated in his pivotal essay "The Root of War is Fear." But almost as important was the *way* he wrote. Through confessional autobiography and lyrical prose-poems — but also ironic social commentary — Merton continually searched for a way to shake his readers free from their conventional thinking and prompt personal and social transformation.

These days Teju Cole, the acclaimed Nigerian American author of the novel *Open City*, has, like Merton, been experimenting with literary form to help sound the alarm about the challenges of our own time. He recently used a technology that wasn't on the monk's radar five decades ago: Twitter.

Merton before, and Cole now, urge us to *see* and *act*.

Toward the end of his life Merton's poems were laced with free verse, verbal collages, made-up dialects ("double-talky witsdom," he called it) and heavy irony. He was consistently on the lookout for a poetics that captured the peculiar dilemmas and resonances of his time. This was true of his last books of poetry (including *Cables to the Ace* and *The Geography of Lograire*) but also specific poems that offered a pointed and ironic illumination of technologized war: "Original Child Bomb" and "Chant to Be Used in Processions Around a Site with Furnaces." Both works referenced World War II — the first focused on the atomic bombing of Hiroshima and Nagasaki, the second on the Holocaust — but they were ultimately trained on the contemporary reader caught in a world threatened by weapons of mass destruction and the systems maintaining them.

"Original Child Bomb" is a flat recitation of the decision and impact of dropping the first atomic bombs, shot through with American sloganeering ("Time is money!")."Chant," delivered in the matter-of-fact voice of a Third Reich concentration camp commander, is a paean to the industrialization of mass death. In the end the narrator refuses to let the morally superior reader off the hook: "Do not think yourself better because you burn up friends and enemies with long-range missiles without ever seeing what you have done."

Merton set for himself the job of vividly clarifying the realities of his world. Now, 50 years later, we face the same task. How can we see and grapple with the challenges of our time, including a comprehensive national security state culture and its penchant for endless war operating far beyond the Cold War binaries with which Merton struggled? And, like Merton, can we find the forms to help us break through our jaded, conditioned vision of things?

This is a tall order, but every once in a while we get glimmers. Teju Cole has gotten us to struggle more concretely with the latest manifestation of our nation's security mania — drone warfare — by recently writing a collection of short stories. Or, rather, *short* short stories: a series of tweets.

Each begins with the opening line of a well-known novel (with the books mostly drawn from the canon of modern European and U.S. literature), including *Mrs. Dalloway* (Virginia Woolf), *Moby Dick* (Herman Melville), *Ulysses* (James Joyce), *Invisible Man* (Ralph Ellison), *The Trial* (Franz Kafka), *Things Fall Apart* (Chinua Achebe) and *The Stranger* (Albert Camus). One at a time he sent these "seven short stories about drones" out into the world:

1. Mrs. Dalloway said she would buy the flowers herself. Pity. A signature strike leveled the florist's.
2. Call me Ishmael. I was a young man of military age. I was immolated at my wedding. My parents are inconsolable.
3. Stately, plump Buck Mulligan came from the stairhead, bearing a bowl of lather. A bomb whistled in. Blood on the walls. Fire from heaven.
4. I am an invisible man. My name is unknown. My loves are a mystery. But an unmanned aerial vehicle from a secret location has come for me.
5. Someone must have slandered Josef K., for one morning, without having done anything truly wrong, he was killed by a Predator drone.
6. Okonkwo was well known throughout the nine villages and even beyond. His torso was found, not his head.
7. Mother died today. The program saves American lives.

If this were a standard literary review, we would want to explore the plot, character development and authorial style of each of these stories. Cole's strategy, of course, short-circuits this analysis. We are left with truncated narratives as much as truncated bodies. The author seems to want us to experience the shock of abrupt physical death but also the collapse of a traditional mechanism for interpreting the meaning of death and the life that precedes it: story-telling in general and literature in particular.

Reflecting on these stories, Cole explained on the radio program *Day 6* that fiction often is designed to "close the empathy gap." In a novel, hundreds of pages are devoted to getting to know characters in their richness, peculiarities, depth and complexity. In contrast, drones ignore the inherent complexity each person possesses and reduce their victims to pixelated objects on a screen thousands of miles away, all without due process and often resulting in civilian deaths. (A recent study conducted by Stanford and New York University, for example, found as many as 881 civilians have been killed by drone strikes in Pakistan.) What, Cole thought, could he do to sense the humanity that is being regularly extinguished in these strikes? What might help us "close the empathy gap"?

He was inspired to use the power of well-known fiction to both generate the expectations of narrative — a story with its own life-cycle, conflicts, insights and resolution is about to begin, in which we will meet a set of characters in all of their richness and idiosyncrasies — and to frustrate it. "Fire from heaven" has suddenly cut this life, and its story, short. Here "short story" means a life shortened, with its potential and meaning abruptly left dangling in the void it was meant to fill.

Storytellers sometimes capture their society in long, sprawling novels or epics. While these are needed, Cole's "tweeted" short stories get at the heart of a woeful horror that is taking hold now, compressing in under 140 characters the millisecond killings carried out by drone aircraft.

The United Nations is beginning an investigation of U.S. and U.K. drone strikes. Unfortunately, it is beginning with the assumption that military drone aircraft are here to stay, and therefore what is needed are rules and regulations, not disarmament. As with previous attempts to deal with many other weapons systems, this represents a colossal failure of imagination.

Thomas Merton and Teju Cole urge us to think beyond this failure. This might involve seeking out the life-stories of those who have been cut down by drones; perhaps it means developing an archive of the as-yet unwritten novel-length narratives revealing the fullness of those killed in these strikes. Perhaps, in that case, the tweet will appropriately give way to the epic novel exposing the intricacies and complexities of each child, woman and man assassinated from the sky.

Merton and Cole have creatively illuminated the reality we are up against. What is also needed is creatively illuminating what is *possible*. Following the impulse of these two visionary artists, we have before us a monumental task: imagining alternatives that do not rely on comprehensive geo-political surveillance and minute-by-minute airborne vigilantes dispatching the presumably guilty; imagining that those under the drones live complicated lives and how they, like us, deserve to continue uninterrupted; and imagining how we can build a powerful people-power movement that will tell a very different kind of story than the foreshortened ones that Teju Cole has so powerfully created.

PART TWO:

Nonviolent Lives Up Close

I had a student at the University of Maryland a while back who wrote a 13-word paper that for both brevity and breadth — the rarest of combinations — has stayed with me: "Question: Why are we violent but not illiterate? Answer: Because we are taught to read.

— Colman McCarthy

Hitlers will come and go. Those who believe that when Hitler dies or is defeated his spirit will die, err grievously. What matters is how we react to such a spirit, violently or nonviolently. If we react violently, we feed that evil spirit. If we act nonviolently, we sterilize it.

— Mohandas Gandhi

Not everything that is faced can be changed, but nothing can be changed until it is faced.

— James Baldwin

16
Vincent Harding: Veteran of Hope
May 21, 2014

Vincent Gordon Harding was both an historian and a maker of history. His calling was to write history, but also to confront history and, in the end, to join with others in breaking the seemingly immutable constrictions of history.

Vincent recently died at the age of 83.

The author of a series of books on the civil rights movement — which he called the Southern Freedom movement — Harding in the 1960s worked with the Student Nonviolent Coordinating Committee, the Southern Christian Leadership Conference, and the Mennonite House in Atlanta, an interracial voluntary service. As part of the Albany, Ga., movement, he was arrested for leading a demonstration at the city hall in 1962. He became a strategist for the movement, and drafted Martin Luther King's historic 1967 anti-war speech "Beyond Vietnam," which King delivered at Riverside Church in New York City one year to the day before his assassination.

Harding had completed his Ph.D. in History at the University of Chicago in 1965 and accepted a teaching position at Spelman College in Atlanta. He tirelessly chronicled the movement in a series of books—including *Hope and History* and *Martin Luther King: The Inconvenient Hero*—and was the senior academic advisor to *Eyes on the Prize*, public television's definitive documentary history of the movement.

Dr. Harding's drive to tell the story of this movement was never a simple matter of buttressing its place in American history—though, in itself, this was a vital undertaking in a nation that tends to erase the experience and achievements of people of color. More important than this for Vincent was a deep need to harvest the improvisational wisdom of what happened. How it

79

caught fire, how it sustained itself, how it wove a resilient canopy of meaning and transformation, often at exceedingly high cost.

Why remember with such tender but steely precision? Because clear-sighted memory can sometimes help us scratch out the tactical lessons and the existential gumption that is needed to continue the monumental work that people like Harding set for themselves back then: creating a multiracial, democratic, egalitarian, and nonviolent society.

Harding eventually became professor of religion and social transformation at Iliff School of Theology in Denver, where he founded Veterans of Hope, a project focused on documenting and learning from struggles for nonviolent change, healing and reconciliation.

Even as he retired from formal teaching, Harding accelerated his efforts for social change. He co-founded the National Council of Elders, crisscrossed the country giving talks and interviews, and made an historic trip to Palestine in late 2012. He and his wife Aljosie Knight were teaching at Pendle Hill Quaker Center for Study and Contemplation in Pennsylvania when he was stricken with an aneurism near his heart, which led to his death in a Philadelphia hospital.

I didn't get to know Harding until later in my own life. Sometime in the 1990s I read his terrific introduction to the reissue of Howard Thurman's 1948 classic, *Jesus and the Disinherited*, a groundbreaking study of Jesus' active nonviolence that had deeply influenced Dr. King's theology and activism. But I didn't meet him until 2009, when he agreed to give the keynote at Pace e Bene Nonviolence Service's 20th anniversary celebration. Rather than delivering a formal address, he made some powerful opening remarks and then threw it open to the rest of us, offering a few choice prompts to facilitate what turned out to be an exhilarating and very rich conversation ranging across the assembly. Throughout this dialogue, Harding's presence — searching, formidable and relentlessly inviting — not only held the space, but also transformed and deepened it.

From then on we stayed in touch. I came to experience, over and over again, the graciousness, clarity, tenacity and nonviolent power Harding had come to — and that he ceaselessly shared with anyone who crossed his path. If the central hallmark of principled nonviolence is an awareness of the oneness of all being, Vincent Harding had thoroughly internalized this. He lived this by endlessly affirming a deep resilient spirit of familial connection with all.

Everyone was sister, everyone was brother. When I would call, his first words always were, "Brother Ken."

There was a stretch where we got on the phone regularly to plot the creation of a new nonviolence project. While nothing ever came of this, the two of us were given the chance to teach a weeklong class together in 2011 at Soka University in Orange County, California. Harding had been the senior advisor on public television's *Eyes on the Prize* series — the magnificent, 12-part program on the civil rights movement — and he decided to use it to anchor the course, which he titled, "Whose Eyes on What Prize Today?" Day after day the small class of 10 students was treated to a powerful opportunity not only to retrace the steps of the Southern Freedom movement — from Montgomery to Mississippi, from Selma to Chicago — but also to sit in the midst of one of the agents of change that had played a critical role in that movement. In our Southern California classroom decades later, Harding communicated the reality of this historic struggle through detailed historical commentary, as well as stirring personal ruminations.

Nothing that week moved me more than his reflections on Birmingham. After setting out a clear exposition of the campaign's goals and tactics for the students — all of whom were born some four decades after these events — Harding shifted gears and unexpectedly got more introspective than usual.

He shared how one morning during the campaign he was

unable to join a line of people as they were moving forward to engage in nonviolent civil disobedience because he was taking care of his six-month-old daughter Rachel. He nevertheless stood tenaciously in the line holding her until the very last possible moment, when he reluctantly moved away from the others. As he recounted this story many years later, Harding's eyes welled up and then he began to openly weep. There seemed to be so much in those tears. The poignancy of his necessary choice; the power of the action itself; the love for his child; the raw emotion at the injustice they were confronting and, in so many ways, were still confronting; and, perhaps, the seismic power of the drama of nonviolent change and the wellspring of feelings it can inspire, washing across the decades — and now, all those years later, touching and inspiring us anew.

The last time I saw Vincent was at the Wild Goose Festival near Asheville, N.C. In addition to making an appearance on the main stage to be interviewed before several thousand people, he joined a more humble gathering in one of the other tents on the premises where a few of us were facilitating a nonviolence training. There was Harding, adrift in the crowd, engaging in small group discussions and taking part in role-plays for the next nonviolent struggle tackling war, poverty and the climate crisis.

My colleague L.R. Berger was a very good friend of Harding's. She tells me that when she spoke to him on the phone during his last days, he said he had profound peace and was embraced in love. "And," she said, "he was hopeful." Harding was a veteran of hope to the end, which may be his greatest gift and example to us all in this time when hope is needed more than ever.

In many forums, Harding advised us not to canonize King. It is too easy to set him apart from the rest of us and thus to ignore the gritty, unfinished business there is to do. King was, as Harding titled his book about the civil rights leader, *The Inconvenient Hero*. In this same spirit, Harding would no doubt assiduously resist his own canonization. Nevertheless, it is right and good to lift our voices in gratitude so that this teacher, mentor and practitioner of active and powerful nonviolence be given his due.

17

Terry Messman: Getting the Story Out

January 24, 2013

Stories are central to our existential job description: making sense of both the world and ourselves. From creation myths to scientific explanations, from political ideologies to the quirky narratives that knead our own amorphous lives into some kind of distinctive shape, stories are essential — not only because they nudge the disconnected bits of reality we face moment to moment into a plausible and graspable form, but because they go to the heart of our identity and purpose.

This goes for navigating our lives. But it also goes for changing the world.

When Dr. Martin Luther King, Jr. says that life poses two fundamental questions —*What are we willing to live for? What are we willing to die for?* — he presupposes a story that makes these questions intelligible. For Dr. King, this story centered on a harrowing and improbable expedition to what he doggedly called the Beloved Community, a world where all human beings will one day sit at the same table, live together in The World House, and make good on the hunch that the moral arc of the universe bends toward justice. This story does not come with a warranty or scientific proof. Instead its truthfulness depends on how far we're willing to go to embellish and inhabit it. This story's power flows, not from its lyrical metaphors, but from its ongoing, risky embodiment.

The monumental challenges we face today — poverty and economic inequality, climate change, military intervention and surveillance, unjust immigration policies, handgun violence, white privilege and many others — resist transformation for many reasons, including the stubbornly enduring frames that keep them in place. The monumental change we need will hinge on a new way of looking at the world, and this in turn will be spurred on by powerful stories that bring that new worldview alive.

Violence draws life from the endless stories that push its power. But things can work the other way too. Stories of the nonviolent option can unexpectedly seep into our right brain, disturb the certitude of the violence operating system, and open breathing space. We are living in a time when, despite the tsunami of violence, we are hearing these counter-narratives more frequently. Part of the reason for this is that there is more nonviolent action than ever. But another is that we are on the lookout for these stories more than ever. When we put on the nonviolence eyewear and start poking we start to see the power of nonviolent change everywhere.

One of our most powerful alternative storytellers is Terry Messman. Messman is the editor of *Street Spirit*, a monthly newspaper published by the American Friends Service Committee that is sold by 100 homeless vendors on the streets of Oakland, Calif. Reporting from "the shelters, back alleys, soup kitchen lines and slum hotels where mainstream reporters rarely or never visit," the newspaper runs stories on homelessness, poverty, economic inequality and the daily grind of human rights violations that poor people face. But *Street Spirit* doesn't simply deliver the grim news of poverty. It also chronicles and raises the visibility of the movement that is dramatically working for human and civil rights, challenging inequality, and demanding — and winning — change. This month's issue, for example, features stories on the challenges and successes of the local anti-foreclosure movement, a campaign countering the erosion of the human rights of homeless people and on affordable housing for the growing senior population. Month after month for the last 17 years *Street Spirit* has been getting the story out on the reality of the structural violence and consequences of poverty, but also on campaigns that are challenging this reality.

Increasingly *Street Spirit* has highlighted the tools of powerful and audacious nonviolent movement-building, with extensive coverage of the Occupy movement and interviews with Erica Chenoweth (on the ground-breaking research that she and Maria Stephan published in their book, *Why Civil Resistance Works* demonstrating that nonviolent strategies are twice as likely to succeed than violent ones) and with nonviolent action campaigner and scholar George Lakey. Last month the newspaper profiled the Positive Peace Warrior Network and one of its key trainers, Kazu Haga, who was trained by Bernard Lafayette and is organizing a growing community of activists grounded in Kingian nonviolence.

By documenting injustice and building the capacity of the movement for justice, *Street Spirit* not only spurs nonviolent action but also has become a form of action itself. Its reporting was instrumental in shutting down the East Bay Hospital in Richmond, Calif., which was a dumping ground for homeless, poor and severely disabled people by nine counties in the region and was responsible for widespread violations of low-income psychiatric patients.

Terry Messman has long integrated telling the story of nonviolent action with action itself. In the late 1970s he was a reporter in Montana sent out to cover a civil disobedience action at a U.S. Air Force base. A lone Lutheran minister had crossed the line at the base and was sitting in the driveway, awaiting arrest. Messman was so moved by this solitary witness that he dropped his reporter's notebook and sat down next to him. He netted six months in federal prison for this action.

Not long after this I met Terry. He was leading a nonviolence training at the Graduate Theological Union in Berkeley, where both of us were then studying. He and several other workshop facilitators were preparing a group to risk arrest at Lawrence Livermore National Laboratory, a nearby facility that had designed 50 percent of the U.S. nuclear arsenal. I was immediately struck by his vision of the power of nonviolence, especially his stress on it being active, audacious, challenging and dramatic. Struck by the picture he painted that morning, I shook off my hesitations about engaging in civil disobedience and took part in the action at the lab, which netted 30 of us a week in the county jail. For the next two years I essentially put my studies on the shelf and took action with Terry and the action group he had helped form named "Spirit Affinity Group" and, in effect, enrolled in Nonviolence 101 with Terry as teacher.

Terry vividly and actively shared with me, and others, the story of nonviolent change, rooted in the vision of Gandhi, Dr. King, Dorothy Day and a rebellious, law-breaking Jesus, whom the theologian and activist John Dear would later characterize as a "one-person crime wave." But Terry's story of the power of nonviolent transformation was rooted not only in studying history but also in a series of actions he had taken throughout the western United States. This story — reinforced by the string of nonviolent actions that we organized and participated in together — was gradually changing me.

After years of anti-nuclear activism, Terry brought this spirit to his work challenging poverty and homelessness in Oakland in the late 1980s. He and others formed the Union of the Homeless that launched an action campaign that included occupying — and winning — an unused federal building and occupying a series of homes that the U.S. Department of Housing and Urban Development had repossessed and was essentially turning over to real estate speculators. They won these homes for poor and homeless families, including a house that Terry and members of the movement (including myself) occupied overnight one time. I will never forget a large Oakland police officer at 4 a.m. kicking open the room I was sound asleep in and dragging me off with the others to jail.

Through it all, Terry was telling the story. Two decades ago I interviewed Terry and his colleagues about their campaign, which by then had mobilized government support to build housing, a childcare center with a Head Start program and a multi-service center supporting homeless people, all run by a nonprofit organization whose board was predominantly homeless people. In one of the interviews Terry said, "We did a four-year series of nonviolent direct actions. And all we did in the early years was say, 'We're going to go to jail for two or three years, and then we're going to have housing.' Which was a totally magical prescription that we just said... And it was really something, that power of belief. We just kept saying that all over the community."

This story — this magical prescription — was key to driving the dramatic actions that created change. Now, all these years later, Terry is still at it as he continues to call out the myriad of ways homeless people are dehumanized and excluded, but also continues to report in a detailed and thoughtful way the stories of the movement that are challenging this dehumanization and exclusion. While *Street Spirit* is Oakland-based, all of us everywhere can all draw new life every month from this powerful platform that's getting the story out for justice and nonviolent transformation.

18

Daniel Berrigan: Marching Orders

May 3, 2016

One is called to live nonviolently, even if the change one works for seems impossible.

— Daniel Berrigan

Fr. Daniel Berrigan has died, and so we have lost our great teacher who, flinty and generous and relentlessly persistent, taught us how to live in a culture of death and madness. "Find some people you can pray with and march with," he said.

Berrigan pronounced this simple sentence at the end of a mesmerizing three-hour conversation he and I had in his Manhattan apartment in late July, 1981. Ricocheting through my unsuspecting soul, this unadorned command dramatically changed my life.

I was a graduate student studying theology at the time, and our wide-ranging exchange was bracing and breathtaking, but the gift that was Dan Berrigan distilled itself into those ten words, compressing spiritual search, community, faith, and action into a pointed moment of decision. Over the next few months I let that invitation circulate within until I was ready to unswervingly say "Yes" to it. Berrigan's simple but profound haiku marked out a way forward for me and, more incisively, beckoned toward a new way of being.

But by the early 1980s, this had been the case for many, many others.

Catholic priest, poet and protester, Dan instructed people everywhere on a life beyond the script handed out by a system that thrives on war and cruelty. We are called to live nonviolence and peacemaking, he told us, with his words—in 40 books and endless poetry—but especially through his communicative action. Using the most powerful language at his disposal, his own vulnerable and creaky body, he unleashed a decades-long conversation with his society with every act of civil disobedience and divine obedience.

There was drama and surprise in these pilgrimages for peace, where he joined others in publicly calling out the well-oiled machinery of war and everything that conspires to keep it running. He wanted to interfere with its smooth functioning, its 24-7 relentlessness, and he found many ways to do this, from burning draft files to hammering on the gadgetry of nuclear annihilation. These vignettes were stunning in the way that Flannery O'Connor's grotesque literary characters were—designed to shock us into recognition and awareness, and to compel us to consider things anew.

Dan stood in a tradition of impresarios of vivid enlightenment, going back to the Hebrew prophets and Jesus—but also the Buddha and a long lineage of mystics and shamans in innumerable cultures and contexts—who have taken it upon themselves to stand in the withering glare of history and declare with their lives a profoundly better way.

I now see that this is what I was looking for when I made my way to his place, that summer day 35 years ago.

Researching the consequences of the nuclear arms race for a book project, I had traveled from California where I was based to the East Coast to visit a number of foreign policy think tanks. No one I spoke with could envision a world free of atomic weapons. At most, they thought we might be able to cut back on nuclear weapons by dramatically increasing conventional ones. Each appointment left me more and more depressed, and finally, when I arrived in New York, I suddenly thought to call Dan. I was in need of some pastoral counseling on the matter of nuclear weapons, and who better to see? We had never met, but he graciously welcomed me to his quarters.

For several hours, he shared with me his vision, which

essentially boiled down to this: "We live in a culture of death — and it is up to us to resist it." There was a lifetime of experience behind these words and I felt the weight of them. Then, as we were coming to the end of our time, I said, "Dan, I'm going back to the West Coast. What can I do for you?" And then he delivered the unexpected missive: "Don't do anything for me. Find some people you can pray with and march with."

On hearing these words, I said to myself, "Me? No, you've got it wrong – I'm not an activist." But for months afterwards, when I was back home in California, Dan's simple phrase kept looping through my brain—challenging me, confronting me, beckoning me. Finally, the following March I found myself attending my first nonviolence training and, then, a few days later, engaging in nonviolent civil disobedience at Lawrence Livermore National Laboratory some 40 miles east of San Francisco, the top-secret facility that had designed 50 percent of the United States' nuclear arsenal. I spent a week in the county jail with thirty other nuclear resisters. It was the beginning of a long journey. Some of those with whom I was incarcerated became close friends and collaborators, including Terry Messman, a theology student who had been deeply inspired by Dan Berrigan.

After I joined a nonviolent action group Terry had helped found – Spirit Affinity Group—he and two other members of the group, Bruce Turner and Pat Runo, made the decision to enter the Catholic Church, deciding to hold the confirmation service at the gates of Livermore Laboratory. We plunged into a huge organizing effort to make this happen. As part of this preparation, Terry wrote to Dan about our plans—whom he had met at a retreat on nonviolence in Sacramento, Calif. a few months before—to which he replied in a letter:

> Your letter and the enclosures would bring tears of joy to a stonier heart than mine. Thank you with all my heart – which I pray is made of bread, not stone.

91

Your plan on entering the Catholic community is surely close to the painful sources and resources that started things Christian – and keep them going. ...civil disobedience is the heart of the matter. Weirdly enough, as John's gospel reminds us, it was the work of healing and raising from the dead, which rang the first tolling of the Savior's fate. It was civilly forbidden to do such things. For the state (and the state religion) claimed the absolute monopoly – on who should live and who should die.

Can any of us claim, as we gaze in stupefaction at the lunar landscape of the nuclear nation state – that such things died with Pilate or Caesar? In the icy gaze of the masters of creation, who, what child, what unborn one, is not expendable?

Into this mad paroxysm, enter the healers – yourselves. So terrifying an act as you envision, so close to the heart of reality! I hope with all my heart that the bishops...will stand at your side. Their presence will confirm not only you, but themselves, with the unction and fire of the Spirit of life. Your own moral clarity will shed light upon their efforts, helping them, as you have been helped, out of the secular quagmire of the official terrorism named deterrence.

Blessed Confirmation to you! You confirm us all, in a madly inhuman time, in a human vocation.

Devotedly, gratefully,
Daniel Berrigan, S.J.

PS. I'm reminded also of your and my conversation in Sacramento, and how our reflections have borne fruit: on entering the church as a public act of witness. Christo gratias!

No bishops joined us that day, but two wonderful priests, Fr. Bill O'Donnell and Fr. Michael Parks, presided in this public ceremony on the edge of this nuclear facility. During the service Terry took as his confirmation name "Daniel," then we joined hundreds of people who prayed and marched to the laboratory, where many were arrested kneeling in the street.

Dan Berrigan's handful of syllables delivered with direct succinctness over thirty years ago in his Manhattan dwelling—"Find some people you can pray with and march with"—hit their mark, and I have done my best to practice them. Following his plain and provocative order, I did as he asked—and my life took an unexpected detour onto a road of nonviolent transformation that I am still, in fits and starts, traveling.

19

Leontine Kelly: Historic Journey
July 5, 2012

Things were proceeding as planned. The annual Good Friday service held across the street from the top-secret nuclear weapons lab had just concluded. Now, as they had for several years in a row, waves of congregants flooded into the intersection to engage in civil disobedience, protesting Lawrence Livermore National Laboratory's design of 50 percent of the United States' atomic arsenal.

Then I saw something that wasn't expected: the preacher at our anti-nuclear service that morning, Bishop Leontine Kelly of the United Methodist Church, was wading out into the street with the others. A Methodist minister sidled up to a few of us and explained that the bishop had suddenly decided to risk arrest. I now saw a troupe of church officials — who had come out to this Northern California nuclear weapons facility simply to be with their bishop — scrambling into the street to join her. A few minutes later, she and her ad hoc affinity group of ecclesiastical bureaucrats were whisked away by the local sheriffs. It was the first time that a bishop had been arrested at the lab.

Bishop Leontine Turpeau Current Kelly was used to "firsts"— in 1984 she became the first African-American women to be elected bishop by any major Christian denomination. She had begun her career as a high school history teacher and then went on to make history herself.

Bishop Kelly recently died at the age of 92.

In 2000 she was elected to the National Women's Hall of Fame, which succinctly declared, "As a spiritual and moral leader, Bishop Kelly advanced the cause of justice in the United States and throughout the world." In addition to working for a world free of the nuclear threat, she tackled issues of violence, poverty, racism, sexuality and illiteracy. She tirelessly advocated for nonviolent change on many fronts, both within her church and throughout society, including opening up the church to gay and lesbian people and in supporting HIV/AIDS ministries. This commitment was rooted in her own experience of her nation's sin of racism and of a church that for much of her life was institutionally segregated — something that her father, also a Methodist minister, had struggled against. As Kelly explained in *Disruptive Christian Ethics: When Racism and Women's Lives Matter* by Traci C. West:

> It is very clear why you have to do battle in relation to a church that is going to take measures to cut anybody out and still call itself church. ... I think that for us as black people, to be drawn into that kind of complete hatred — and that is what it is, hatred — violates our own history and the way God has worked with us.
>
> I have to go back to the context of our home when I was growing up, and to issues of race, when talking about gay rights issues... I remember when my father came back from the Uniting Conference [in 1939]. Now that meeting was about the last real schism over slavery, when the Methodist Church North and the Methodist Church South had split over slavery. ... My father went to that conference when the Central Jurisdiction was established as a compromise [institutionally segregating the Methodist Church]. For the white southern church to come back and be united with the north, they would not accept the inclusion of blacks. ... I remember when he came back and we were having dinner and I asked my father, "Papa, why do you stay in this segregated church? You can be Christian without being Methodist."
>
> My father's answer was, "You don't win a battle by leaving the battlefield. You've got to stay there. We have

more battling to do because if the Central Jurisdiction is going to ever be dissolved it is going to have to come from within. If I am going to be a Christian, I am going to be where I can battle. The church cannot be Christian without us."

The Central Jurisdiction was dissolved in 1968, but only after numerous nonviolent battles. Leontine Kelly rooted her support for a radically inclusive church and society in her experience of the long-term struggle for justice, something that was vividly brought home to her as she grew up in Cincinnati where her mother founded a chapter of the Urban League and the parsonage where her family lived had been a station on the Underground Railroad.

These foundations for a ministry dedicated to advocating justice and peace were reinforced at different points in her life, including the impact of Martin Luther King Jr.'s work in Richmond, Virginia, when she was still a public school teacher. A dozen years ago at a King holiday celebration in Oakland Kelly shared her memory of this encounter:

She recalled watching at a lunch counter sit-in a few days after King came to Richmond, when an angry young man flicked his cigarette down the blouse of a protester planted at the counter. Kelly said the victimized woman "had been taught how to take it in the name of God by Martin Luther King Jr. when he was there. Tears ran down her face but I had the sense that they were more for the young man who flicked the cigarette than for any pain she had."

Then, as her own vocation as church reformer often prompted her to do, she followed this recollection with an application to the faith community: "[King's] lesson... was that every religious institution 'that takes up space in a community' should be used to improve the lives of those who live there."

For Leontine Kelly, this community extended globally. In 1995, on the 50th anniversary of the atomic bombings of Hiroshima and Nagasaki, Bishop Kelly joined hundreds of peace advocates at the Nevada Test Site to renew the call for an end to the proliferation of nuclear weapons. As one of those who joined her in that August heat, I continue to be deeply moved by the way she carried on her nonviolent battles for the well-being of all.

20
David Hartsough:
An Ordinary, Extraordinary Life
November 12, 2014

Years ago, my friend Anne Symens-Bucher would regularly punctuate our organizing meetings with a wistful cry, "I just want to live an ordinary life!" Anne ate, drank and slept activism over the decade she headed up the Nevada Desert Experience, a long-term campaign to end nuclear testing at the Nevada Test Site. After a grueling conference call, a mountainous fundraising mailing, or days spent at the edge of the sprawling test site in 100-degree weather, she and I would take a deep breath and wonder aloud how we could live the ordinary, nonviolent life without running ourselves into the ground.

What we didn't mean was: "How do we hold on to our radical ideals but also retreat into a middle-class cocoon?" No, it was something like: "How can we stay the course but not give up doing all the ordinary things that everyone else usually does in this one-and-only life?" Somewhere in this question was the desire to not let who we are — in our plain old, down-to-earth ordinariness — get swallowed up by the blurring glare of the 24/7 activist fast lane.

These ruminations came back to me as I plunged into the pages of David Hartsough's recent memoir, *Waging Peace: Global Adventures of a Lifelong Activist.* David has been a friend for 30 years, and over that time I've rarely seen him pass up a chance to jump into the latest fray with both feet — something he'd been doing long before we met, as his book attests. For nearly six decades he's been organizing for nonviolent change — with virtually every campaign, eventually getting tangled up with one risky nonviolent action after another. Therefore, one might be tempted to surmise that David is yet another frantic activist on the perennial edge of burnout. Just *reading* his book, with its relentless kaleidoscope of civil resistance on many continents, can be dizzying — what must it have been like to *live* it? If anyone would qualify for *not* living the ordinary life, it would seem to be David Hartsough.

As I finished his 250-page account, however, I drew a much different conclusion. I found myself thinking that maybe David has figured it out — maybe he's been living the ordinary life all along.

Which is not to downplay the technicolor drama of his journey. Since meeting Martin Luther King, Jr. as a teenager in the mid-1950s, David has been actively part of many key nonviolent movements over the last half-century: the civil rights movement, the anti-nuclear testing movement, the movement to end the Vietnam War, the U.S. Central America peace movement, the anti-apartheid movement, and the movements to end the U.S. wars in Iraq and Afghanistan. In recent years he has helped found the Nonviolent Peaceforce and a new global venture to end armed conflict, World Beyond War.

This book is jammed with powerful stories from these efforts — from facing down with nonviolent love a knife-wielding racist during an eventually successful campaign to desegregate a lunch-counter in Arlington, Va., in 1960, to paddling canoes into the way of a U.S. military ship bound for Vietnam; from meeting with President John Kennedy to urge him to spark a "peace race" with the Soviet Union, to being threatened with arrest in Red Square in Moscow for calling for nuclear disarmament there; from confronting the death squad culture in Central America and the Philippines to watching his good friend, Vietnam veteran Brian Willson, get mowed down by a U.S. Navy munitions train.

These are just a few of the innumerable vignettes of David's peacemaking around the world. But there is much more to David's life story than these intense scenes of nonviolent conflict.

Much of this book recounts how the foundations of his career as an agent of nonviolent change were laid, slowly and organically. His decision to give his life to peacemaking was shaped by the inspiration of his parents, who were both actively involved in building a better world, and by a series of experiences in which he witnessed the impact of violence and injustice, but also at the same time met a series of remarkable organizers who were not content to simply wring their hands at such destruction, including the likes of civil rights movement luminaries Bayard Rustin and Ralph Abernathy.

Most powerful of all, David set out on a series of illuminating explorations, with long stints in the Soviet Union, Cuba and a then-divided Germany. Everywhere he met people who turned out to be complicated, beautiful and often peace-loving human beings. His nonviolence — and resistance to war — was strengthened by seeing for himself the people his own government deemed "the enemy."

In Berlin — a city split between the East and West after World War II, but not yet separated by the wall the Soviets would build — he took classes on both sides of the divide and experienced up close what the "us" versus "them" of violence feels like: "In the mornings [at the university in the East] I would challenge the Communist propaganda and be labeled a 'capitalist war-monger,'" he writes. "In the afternoons, at the university in the West, when I challenged their propaganda I was called a 'Communist conspirator.' I thought I must be doing something right if neither side appreciated my questions! I didn't consider myself any of these things: capitalist, war-monger, Communist, conspirator." Instead, he was a nonviolent activist challenging the confining labels that are used to foment the separations that fuel and legitimate violence and injustice.

David has rooted his lifelong pilgrimage of peace in a simple conviction: that all life is precious. He has helped spark and build one campaign after another when that preciousness is forgotten or undermined.

At the same time, he's recognized that such a nonviolent life extends to himself. This is where the ordinary life comes in.

David and his spouse Jan live a simple life interweaving family time (including with their children and grandchildren, who live downstairs from them) with building a better world. They are activists, but they rarely let organizing keep them from taking a hike in the mountains or a walk along the seashore. They are regulars at the local Quaker meeting. For decades they have been sharing their home with countless friends, who are often invited to the songfests that they frequently organize in their living room. When I stay with them in San Francisco, there is always a bike ride through Golden Gate Park to be had or time to be spent at a garden a few blocks away with its dazzling profusion of azaleas. Rather than giving short shrift to the fullness of life, David has found a way to live, as we say today, holistically.

David's life qualifies as "ordinary," though, not only because it knits together many dimensions of everyday realities, but because it has dissolved the artificial boundary between "activism" and "non-activism." All of life is an opportunity to celebrate and defend its preciousness, and this impulse gets worked out seamlessly in both watering the plants and getting carted off to a police van after engaging in nonviolent resistance at a nuclear weapons laboratory. Nonviolent action is a seamless part of the rhythm of life. It is a crucial part of the ordinary life. Once enough of us see this and fold it into the rest of our life, its ordinariness will become even more evident than it is now. This was Gandhi's feeling — nonviolence and nonviolent resistance is a normal part of being human — and David has taken this assumption up in a clear and thoughtful way.

Anne Symens-Bucher reports that she's increasingly living the ordinary life — she's developed a powerful example of it called Canticle Farm in Oakland, Calif. And I feel I'm getting closer to it day by day. But if you want to read a page-turner that reveals how one person has been doing it for the last 50 years, get hold of a copy of David Hartsough's autobiography, *Waging Peace: Global Adventures of a Lifelong Activist.*

21
Daniel Ellsberg:
Determined Lifelong Resistance
July 11, 2013

Daniel Ellsberg recently published a thoughtful opinion piece in the *Washington Post* on Edward Snowden's decision to leave the country after releasing information about the National Security Agency's massive surveillance program. Ellsberg highlights how Snowden's self-imposed exile is itself a critically important nonviolent action that is multiplying and extending his original act of conscience. Nonviolent resistance is not confined to the specific, isolated, dramatic act, Ellsberg seems to be suggesting. It opens opportunities for new action, and can come to be seen as part of an ever expanding drama, with many acts and episodes, all potentially furthering the opportunity for nonviolent change.

This speaks to Edward Snowden's case — but it might apply even more to Ellsberg himself.

Releasing the Pentagon Papers in 1971 was an historic act. Since then Ellsberg has relentlessly built on and expanded upon this particular nonviolent action in innumerable ways. Retirement doesn't seem to apply to the job of making the world a better place, as Ellsberg proves almost daily.

Snowden has been criticized for fleeing the country. Some have compared him disapprovingly to Ellsberg, who, after leaking the Pentagon Papers to the *New York Times* and other papers in 1971, came forward and was eventually tried in a court of law. In his piece, Ellsberg challenged this negative comparison by carefully illuminating his own case in his fervent support of Snowden.

After the *New York Times* began publishing the documents demonstrating how the U.S. government misled the public about the roots and conduct of the war in Vietnam, Ellsberg went underground so that, once the paper was enjoined by federal injunction to halt publication, he could continue to feed copies to other news agencies. Eventually, 17 papers across the United States got the information out, but this would not have happened if he had turned himself in immediately.

Ellsberg also points out that he was free on bail both before and during his trial, which allowed him to crisscross the country to speak to the media and the general public to magnify the meaning and implications of the Pentagon Papers. Though he was prosecuted under U.S. espionage laws, and faced 115 years in federal prison, he was released on his own recognizance and was free to engage in a conversation with American society about the war. America, he says, is a very different place today. Snowden would likely have been sequestered as soon as he surfaced. There would be no extended conversation with the country once he turned himself in to the authorities.

"Snowden believes that he has done nothing wrong. I agree wholeheartedly," Ellsberg writes. "More than 40 years after my unauthorized disclosure of the Pentagon Papers, such leaks remain the lifeblood of a free press and our republic. One lesson of the Pentagon Papers and Snowden's leaks is simple: secrecy corrupts, just as power corrupts." Ellsberg goes on to say that what Snowden "has given us is our best chance — if we respond to his information and his challenge — to rescue ourselves from out-of-control surveillance that shifts all practical power to the executive branch and its intelligence agencies."

The essay from which these excerpts are quoted is the kind of gift Ellsberg has been placing in our hands for decades: an intelligent, documented and detailed assessment that unpacks, illuminates and reveals the particulars at hand — in this case, the risky business Snowden has taken on — but always at the same time aimed at plumbing the dangerous waters into which both the nation and the world seem to be headed.

While Ellsberg sometimes draws on his own experience as a uniquely positioned whistleblower in making his argument — this is especially the case in his superb book *Secrets: A Memoir of Vietnam and the Pentagon Papers* — his blogs, essays and books are not about reliving the increasingly distant past but about grappling with the present. Each new essay or speech sparkles with an urgency about what we are up against *now*, whether that's the ever-present threat of a U.S. invasion of Iran, the ongoing threat of nuclear weapons, or the threat of comprehensive surveillance — and calls us to a considered understanding of both the dangers we face and the options before us.

To me, these innumerable dispatches of wisdom — analytic, principled and often somber — are of a piece with the other way Ellsberg has tried to get our attention over the past four decades: nonviolent civil disobedience.

"After leaking the Pentagon Papers, you could have sat on your laurels," I once said to him in an interview. "Why didn't you?" He looked at me with bewilderment. Though such a thing might have occurred to someone else — taking such a risky step, after all, is trouble enough for a lifetime — for him the work wasn't finished. In fact, releasing the papers seemed to release something in him, so that he plunged feet first into the roiling waters of nonviolent movements using the most powerful symbol he had at his disposal to back up his words and his analysis: his own vulnerable body.

The interview we did, for example, concerned his active participation in the waves of nonviolent action at the Nevada Test Site in the 1980s. The United States detonated nuclear weapons at the site north of Las Vegas on average once every 18 days beginning in 1951. Ellsberg took part in the nonviolent resistance organized by Nevada Desert Experience and other organizations to stop this, but he also participated in riskier actions than simply crossing the line at the facility's entrance. In 1985 he and a couple of members of Greenpeace walked deep into the site just before a nuclear device was scheduled to be detonated. Via walkie-talkie, they made contact with the test site authorities that they were in the area and that they should not follow through with the test. Not only was the test delayed, Ellsberg managed to communicate with some friends in Congress who used the news of this action to help pass a bill in the House calling for an end to testing. (It was eventually killed in the Senate.) These actions contributed to those by many others in the United States and around the world to establish the Comprehensive Test Ban Treaty in the early 1990s.

But there are so many other times when he was arrested for nonviolent civil disobedience: at an historic action when hundreds were arrested at the CIA headquarters; as part of the campaign at Concord Naval Weapons Station where his friend, Brian Willson, was run down by a train carrying arms bound for Central America; and innumerable protests against the Persian Gulf War and the later wars in Iraq and Afghanistan. He has been arrested at the White House and at Red Square in Moscow.

One of my favorite examples is the yearlong campaign at Rocky Flats, the facility outside Denver that manufactured the plutonium pits used in nuclear arms. He and others took part in waves of resistance month after month. Dubbed the "Rocky Flats Truth Force," the protesters sat on a strategic railroad spur to "stop the arms race in its tracks" and interfere with the smooth functioning of nuclear weapons assembly and production. Many were arrested and tried, including Ellsberg. About this trial and the testimony he gave during it, Ellsberg later wrote, "As a former official speaking on so many matters which so many officials have concealed, denied and lied about over the years, I was glad to have the opportunity in court to testify to my knowledge and beliefs. I revealed the Pentagon Papers because I believed that decades of secrecy surrounding official decision making in Vietnam, by promoting public ignorance and passivity, had prolonged a needless and wrongful war and threatened the survival of our democracy."

The ongoing threats to our democracy persist, and Ellsberg continues to sound the alarm with his words and with his body, including regularly engaging in nonviolent civil disobedience. Like Edward Snowden, Daniel Ellsberg persists with peaceful but determined resistance. He reminds us that at any point in our lives there's work to be done.

22

Anne Symens-Bucher:
Lessons in the Desert

April 19, 2012

It remains the most bombed real estate on the planet.

The Nevada Test Site — recently renamed the Nevada National Security Site — is 1,360 square miles of sprawling desert north of Las Vegas. A nuclear weapon was detonated there on average every eighteen days from 1951 through 1992.

In the 1980s the spiritually-rooted Nevada Desert Experience (NDE) launched a campaign with the audacious goal of ending this practice. For the next decade its effort gained traction, with thousands of people from across the U.S. and around the world converging on the site's southern gate to protest, pray and engage in nonviolent civil disobedience. Other organizations, including the American Peace Test (APT) and Greenpeace, joined NDE in this struggle. In 1988, three thousand people were arrested in a ten-day action organized by APT at the Nevada Test Site.

A founder of NDE, Anne Symens-Bucher spent years in Nevada building this effort to end nuclear weapons testing. She was part of a group of Catholic sisters, priests lay people and others who organized a forty-day vigil at the site in 1982 to mark the 800th anniversary of the birth of St. Francis of Assisi, which they named the "Lenten Desert Experience." In 1983 a shorter vigil was organized, then in 1984 Lenten Desert Experience III was hosted from April 1 through April 30, 1984 at the gates of the test site. No nuclear tests were conducted during the month-long vigil; they resumed three days after the action concluded. The fact that no nuclear bombs were detonated during that month got them thinking about continuing their effort; a number of the key organizers, including Symens-Bucher, decided that the

108

momentum existed for the development of an ongoing campaign at the test site. Nevada Desert Experience was born.

Against all odds, the Comprehensive Test Ban Treaty (CTBT) was established in 1992. NDE and many other organizations built a global movement that mobilized people-power on every continent to create the conditions for an end to nuclear testing. One hundred eighty-two nations became signatories. Though Bill Clinton signed the treaty in 1996, the U.S. Senate has yet to ratify it. Nevertheless, the United States has maintained a moratorium on full-blown nuclear tests for over two decades. While the nuclear threat is as alive as ever, the world is no longer subject to the numbing horror of this dress rehearsal for Armageddon and its environmental, political and moral fallout.

NDE is now over 30 years old. Since the promulgation of the CTBT, people within the organization have periodically wondered if it should declare victory and close up shop. The answer has been a resounding "No." NDE has stayed put, with a focus on the nuclear and non-nuclear projects that continue at the test site and the dramatic surge in drone warfare coordination at nearby Creech Air Force Base. At the same time, it continues to vigorously support the Western Shoshone nation in its struggle with the U.S. government, which violated the 1863 Treaty of Ruby Valley by confiscating Western Shoshone and Southern Paiute land to build the site. In addition to a weekly vigil, NDE organizes a "Sacred Peace Walk" from Las Vegas to the test site every spring, and an annual commemoration of the atomic bombings of Hiroshima and Nagasaki in August.

From the vantage point of three decades, there are a couple of lessons that may shed light on the challenges and opportunities of building movements for change today.

First, this movement did not begin with a clear strategy. It was founded by a handful of people who ventured into the desert to bear witness to present and potentially future nuclear destruction. Franciscan sisters, brothers and lay people seeking a way to mark the 800th birthday of St. Francis of Assisi followed their hearts to the test site, where for 40 days they maintained a presence during the Christian season of Lent. Their witness culminated in nonviolent civil disobedience as 19 people crossed onto this top-secret nuclear facility and were arrested.

Several years ago, I published a book about this movement—*Pilgrimage Through a Burning World: Spiritual Practice and Nonviolent Protest*—and a recurring perception among the organizers I interviewed was that NDE lacked a strategy, and that this had hurt the effort. What I began to appreciate, however, was that a different kind of strategic thinking had been at work. This was one not based on a SWOT analysis or models of community organizing, but on relentless persistence: ongoing presence, action and occupation. (For example, a Peace Camp was established outside the gates of the facility where people would stay for long stretches of time, including a former defense worker, Art Casey, who spent two years there.)

This continuity established a growing legitimacy and visibility, which attracted people to this largely invisible site at a time when the emerging anti-nuclear weapons movement, stoked by the Reagan administration's military buildup, was looking for tangible and concrete focus. Once people woke up to the fact that the government was still exploding nuclear weapons in the western part of the United States — and had not stopped in 1962 when the tests went below ground — people wanted to get involved, and a growing number of them thought about going out to the desert for themselves.

What helped translate this longing into making the long drive, boarding a plane or hitchhiking from the nearest interstate on-ramp was the peaceful atmosphere that NDE sought to create from the beginning. Nuclear weapons symbolize and embody mega-violence. What is needed, the founders reasoned, is not more violence but mega-nonviolence. This involved engaging in a Gandhian experiment with truth, which for them meant striking a balance between resistance and openness in their relationship with test site personnel and the local sheriffs.

They didn't think of this strategically — in fact, they thought of this as a spiritual discipline — but in a strange way it turned out to be hyper-strategic. Over months and then years, an insistence on transforming "us versus them" thought and action established relationships at the test site that reduced the likelihood of violent interactions with employees and law enforcement. This, in turn, created a climate that attracted many more people to the campaign than a violent one likely would have. This relatively peaceful atmosphere, created at the edge of a nuclear firing range, emboldened a growing number of people to risk arrest and to face the consequences.

This atmosphere was not inevitable. It could have gone very differently, depending on the predilections of either side. The protesters had asked for a meeting with the director of the test site beforehand, which had turned out to be a powerful encounter. And from the very first day they took action at the site, they were scrupulous about maintaining the spirit of nonviolence. At the same time, the head sheriff who dealt with them was fairly new to police work and made it clear, through his words and actions, that he would respect the right of people to protest.

NDE had no illusions about the evil that the test site, and the larger nuclear weapons system, represented. At the same time, it held to what the late feminist writer Barbara Deming called the two hands of nonviolence: noncooperation with violence and steadfast regard for the opponent as a human being.

For the first year or two, the local county court meted out punishments in the range of a few weeks to several months, but as the numbers increased, the county threw up its hands. It did not have the resources to prosecute and jail an increasingly steady stream of anti-nuclear advocates. It announced that, except under highly unusual circumstances, it would issue citations but not act on them. This opened the floodgates. Soon, large numbers of people were making pilgrimage to the test site and engaging in nonviolent civil disobedience.

For some, this meant that risking arrest at NTS had little value. Anne Symens-Bucher saw it differently. For her, NDE actions became a kind of school or training ground for civil disobedience. The peaceful atmosphere that NDE fostered became a place where many people risked arrest for the first time. It prepared them to work for an end to nuclear testing back in their own communities, including taking nonviolent action there.

A few years after this movement began, Symens-Bucher described the vision of NDE's experiment in truth:

I have become wholly convinced that something is happening at the Test Site which is difficult – if not impossible – to articulate. It is, however, experienced. I have witnessed time and again, people participating in the vigil and going home changed. Something is happening at the Test Site, and it is happening not because we are organizationally efficient, but in spite of the fact that we are not. People of faith and goodwill are being drawn together in the Nevada desert and together they are bringing life and goodness and re-creation to a place of evil, death, and destruction. The location is perfect: the vastness of the desert, the desert in all its stark beauty. It is a beauty which is appreciated slowly, over a period of time … It is conducive to prayer, meditation, soul-searching, purification. It is as if people are able, in the setting of the desert, to reach down into their depths and discover what is good and what is the gift in themselves and in each other. This goodness, this gift, this power, this life-force collectively brought forth, becomes tangible. Bonds are formed. Community happens. Love is made real. And out of this love, we are able to confront the evil in the desert. Out of this love we are able to heal ourselves, each other and the earth upon which we stand. Because of this love, nuclear weapons testing will end.

And end it did. NDE's commitment to ongoing action, in season and out, contributed to a political groundswell, which, as I have traced elsewhere, was key to the establishment of the CTBT and a U.S. moratorium on testing. This shift was the result of many important clear and defined strategies, which are crucial to the success of all movements. But it was also the result of NDE's nonviolent "unstrategic strategy."

23

Brian Willson: "We Are Not Worth More, They Are Not Worth Less"

September 1, 2011

On September 1, 1987 Vietnam veteran Brian Willson joined a handful of peacemakers on the railroad tracks at Concord Naval Weapons Station to begin what they envisioned as a forty-day fast and vigil to protest arm shipments from this Northern California military base to U.S.-backed forces in Central America.

Instead, a 900-ton munitions train, traveling at three times the legal speed limit, plowed into Brian and dragged him under. Standing a few feet away, I saw him turn over and over again like a rag doll and then, as the never-slowing train rumbled on toward a nearby security gate, sprawling in the track bed, a huddled mass of blood.

Miraculously, Brian survived—thanks, largely, to the tourniquets applied by his then-wife, Holly Rauen, a professional nurse—though both legs were sheared off and his skull was fractured.

Brian recently published *Blood on the Tracks: The Life and Times of S. Brian Willson,* a new autobiography available from PM Press. This book does not simply recount a horrifying event from long ago. It offers, more importantly, a vivid example of a still-unfolding pilgrimage for peace that turns on a burning question: "What is my responsibility to make peace and challenge murderous violence in a direct and meaningful way?"

At a critical turning point in his life, Brian allowed this question in and everything changed. Of course, this question is not Brian's alone. It is meant for each of us in the midst of the storm of horrific violence that continually bears down on our planet and its inhabitants.

Brian's memoir recounts his journey from childhood in upstate New York—born on the Fourth of July, he enthusiastically shared his family's pro-military and anti-communist convictions—to his decision to go to law school and then his being drafted and being sent to Vietnam as an Air Force captain, where two incidents changed his life.

One was a rocket attack where his life was saved by a quick-thinking companion who pushed him to the ground and out of the way of the blast. Though they survived, another soldier was blown to bits a few feet away. The second even more clearly seared his soul. He had been sent out to do damage assessment of US bombing raids on villages and found a blackened mess that used to be huts, littered with bodies:

> My first thought was that I was witnessing an egregious, horrendous mistake. The "target" was no more than a small fishing and rice farming community. The "village" was smaller than a baseball playing field. The Mekong Delta region is completely flat, and the modest houses in its hamlets are built on small mounds among rice paddies. As with most settlements, this one was undefended — we saw no anti-aircraft guns, no visible small arms, no defenders of any kind. The pilots who bombed this small hamlet flew low-flying planes, probably the A-37Bs, and were able to get close to the ground without fear of being shot down, thus increasing the accuracy of their strafing and bombing. They certainly would have been able to see the inhabitants, mostly women with children taking care of various farming and domestic chores...The buildings were virtually flattened by explosions or destroyed by fire. I didn't see any inhabitant on his or her feet. Most were ripped apart from bomb shrapnel and Gatling machine gun wounds, blackened from napalm burns, many not discernable as to gender, and the majority were obviously children.

115

I began sobbing and gagging. I couldn't fathom what I was seeing, smelling, thinking. I took a few faltering steps to my left, only to find my way blocked by the body of a young woman lying at my feet. She had been clutching three small, partially blackened children when she apparently collapsed. I bent down for a closer look and stared, aghast, at the woman's open eyes. The children were motionless, blackened blood drying on their bullet and shrapnel-riddled bodies. Napalm had melted much of the woman's face, including her eyelids, but as I was focused on her face, it seemed to me that her eyes were staring at me.

She was not alive. But her eyes and my eyes met for one moment that shot like a lightning bolt through my entire being. Over the years I have thought of her so much I have given her the name, "Mai Ly."

I was startled when Bao, who was several feet to my right, asked why I was crying. I remember struggling to answer. The words that came out astonished me. "She is my family," I said, or something to that effect. I don't know where those words came from. I wasn't thinking rationally. But I felt, in my body, that she and I were one. Bao just smirked, and said something about how satisfied he was with the bombing "success" in killing "communists." I did not reply. I had nothing to say. From that moment on, nothing would ever be the same for me.

Thus began a deep transformation, which led him in the 1980s to notice with deep alarm the connection between what he had experienced in Vietnam and the Reagan administration's war in Central America. He traveled to the region and saw a vivid parallel between the two conflicts, especially the wanton attack on civilians, and became convinced that he had to take action.

"We are not worth more, they are not worth less," he declared, and joined the Veterans Fast for Life on the steps of the US Capitol in 1986, where he and three other former members of the US military fasted for 47 days. One year later, he and others formed Nuremberg Actions—named after the principles of international law enunciated in the wake of the Nuremberg tribunal following World War II that defined crimes against humanity and the responsibility and complicity in such crimes—and organized a forty day fast at Concord in which he and others planned to block weapons trains. A Freedom of Information Request had yielded concrete evidence that ships leaving this base were carrying 500-pound bombs, white phosphorus, and millions of rounds of ammunition, and Brian wanted to stop such shipments in their tracks.

He expected the train to stop, at which point he would be removed and arrested—in effect compelling the military to demonstrate the kind of care that should also be accorded to those at the other end of the line in Nicaragua and El Salvador. Instead, the government ran the train (in spite of the clear communication with the Navy over the prior ten days), thus dramatizing with palpable clarity what those at the end of the line faced every day.

There are many lessons from Brian's journey. One is the importance of "finding your own tracks and taking a stand there," as he has often said. A catchphrase we used at the time held that "Stopping the war starts here"—stopping it at a weapons base, but also in many, many other places. Brian did so by taking this action "in person": using the most powerful symbol at his disposal, his vulnerable, resilient, determined, and spirited body.

We can do this, too. This is not to say that we are all called to sit on train tracks (such action requires much discernment and training). But there are many places to stand nonviolently, withdrawing our consent and pointing our communities, our societies, and even ourselves in a new direction. The world begins to change when we find this place.

September 6, 2012

Last weekend fifty of us who had been part of that original witness at the Concord Naval Weapons Station—and the eight-year Nuremberg Actions Campaign that followed—gathered with Brian at the base 30 miles east of San Francisco. Like the others, I was drawn to mark an event that had profound personal significance—my life falls into two parts: before the incident at the Concord tracks and after it—but also one that resounded with the power of nonviolent social change. From many parts of the country, we made a pilgrimage to this place fraught with trauma but also, paradoxically, with transformative energy.

A pilgrimage is a journey to a meaningful place. As Jean and Wallace Clift stress in their book *The Archetype of Pilgrimage* some people go on pilgrimage to experience a place of power. Others undertake a pilgrimage to answer an inner call or to reclaim lost or abandoned or forgotten parts of themselves. Still others become pilgrims to get outside the normal routine of life so something new can happen. Each of these motivations, it seems, played a part in last week's gathering.

Experiencing a place of power. When human beings stand for justice it is transformative for themselves and at times transformative for their society. But it is also, I believe, transformative for the place where such a struggle occurs. When I first visited the California Central Valley, I was awash in its sacredness: not only because it helps feed America, but because it is here that the migrant poor formed the United Farm Workers and took a stand for dignity and human rights. Similarly, the site where Brian Willson (and hundreds of others after him) took a stand is a place of meaning bearing enduring witness to the power of nonviolent love in action. When we live in a society that defines power as domination and control backed by violence, we are healed and transformed when we make contact with a different kind of power: the power of compassion, connection,

118

community—and the willingness to face the consequences for putting this power into action.

Reclaiming lost or abandoned or forgotten parts of ourselves. Returning to the Concord tracks gave us an opportunity to remember what went down there and, by remembering, to renew our passion and commitment to a world where everyone matters. We live in a world that strenuously works to erase our history of nonviolent resistance. To journey to this place (and many scenes of nonviolent struggle) is a process of contesting this erasure. As Brian Willson said when contemplating the importance of observing this anniversary, "Those who control the present control the past, and those who control the past control the future. As memory is obliterated, people possess no frame of reference for assessing present policies. Thus, imperial history repeats itself over and over." By remembering, we reclaim these forgotten dimensions of ourselves, but also of our society.

Answering an inner call. The longing that brought us to Concord in the first place burns within us still: the hope for a world where the nonviolent option is the default, with the follow-on call: *translate this into reality with creativity and relentless persistence.* Throughout our time together last weekend, we mulled on this question: "Where will this desire and call take us now?"

Getting outside the normal routine of life so something new can happen. The work for nonviolent change means peeling away the scripts, patterns and habits of domination and violence with which we have been formed. This was symbolized by some of us dropping what we were doing in the rest of our lives and gathering to see a new way forward together. This is true for us as individuals, but it is the vocation of social movements to do this for one's society. Nuremberg Actions did this by rising from the ashes of the violence of September 1987 to build an enormously powerful campaign, with trains being blocked on a virtually daily basis for several years. The Occupy movement could glean much wisdom from the travails and triumphs of this multi-year effort.

119

All of these dimensions of pilgrimage crystalized in two images at our recent gathering. First, Brian Willson, standing on his two artificial legs, erupting in dance as one of the musicians leads the gathering in song. Second, the sacred journey we made from the rally site to the tracks where Brian was run down all those years ago. Poignant. Heartfelt. But also a moment of recommitment in a world where people are being run down by the train of history— now, often, in the guise of swarming drones—throughout the world. At this hauntingly abysmal place, the energy of connection and potential and new action hummed through us, with most of us sensing that the next pilgrimage is just ahead.

24

John Dear: The Power of Nonviolence
June 16, 2016

I propose that each one of us reject violence as a way of life and consciously choose to live a life of nonviolence; teach others the way of nonviolence; and do our part to build a global grassroots movement of nonviolence. This is our only alternative in the face of our global illness, our common insanity, our committed violence. We need to work toward global healing, common sanity, and committed nonviolence.

– John Dear

A quarter of a century ago, as President George H. W. Bush was mustering the world for war against Iraq, I first had a chance to work with John Dear. We both happened to be in the San Francisco Bay Area at the time. I was fresh from Washington, DC, where for three years I had been the national coordinator of the Pledge of Resistance – a movement of nonviolent direct action organized to end US wars then at fever pitch in Central America—and he was already a globe-trotting peace activist and budding author.

We plunged into organizing a raft of marches and civil disobedience actions with a couple of ad hoc groups. We helped fill St. Mary's Catholic Cathedral in San Francisco to the brim on the eve of the war where we joined with thousands of our sisters and brothers of many traditions and faiths to pray that war be averted – and prayed that, if not, we would be prepared to pursue peace if our government wouldn't.

The United States invaded Iraq on Dr. Martin Luther King, Jr.'s birthday, and we spent every day for weeks in the streets taking part in nonviolent action as part of the larger national and international movement. In the midst of all of it, John was a great collaborator and partner – energetic, creative and relentlessly persistent.

Many powerful vignettes come back to me now—including a wonderfully long talk we had together in court waiting for an arraignment after one of the many arrests that month—but perhaps the single most vivid moment was the procession we organized up one of the main streets in San Francisco where, inspired by Dr. King's example, hundreds of us would kneel in the traffic-filled streets to pray, then resume our march, then pray again. We walked solemnly a few miles to the gate of the Presidio, which then was still a U.S. Army base near the Golden Gate Bridge. I recall our speaking to the assembled at the east gate, which was heavily fortified by troops. The soldiers wouldn't let us pass into the fort, so scores of us walked a few feet down a nearby hill and then floated, almost magically, over the base's stone wall.

When we landed on the other side we again knelt. The soldiers were young and nervous and we did our best to soothe them with our words and our composure. Eventually they arrested us and dispatched us to a holding cell somewhere.

For the past twenty-five years we have been in touch. John has gone on to become a very prolific writer – he has published 32 books at this point and tells me he is usually working on six at a time. He has made an enormous contribution to our understanding of Jesus' nonviolence and the necessity of actively working for the healing of the planet and its far-flung beings— something he has taken seriously in his own life by taking nonviolent action on a regular basis in many settings.

In 2013 John became part of Pace e Bene Nonviolence Service, where he joined our circle of change-makers in dreaming about a new, long-term movement for a culture of peace and nonviolence free from war, poverty, racism, environmental destruction and the epidemic of violence. Like many of us, John had focused for many years on single issue organizing. Together we came to see the need for an overarching effort toward a new, nonviolent world, connecting the dots between all the facets of violence that plague our world, but also connecting the dots between the innumerable initiatives working for a more just, peaceful and sustainable earth. Campaign Nonviolence was born.

In September 2014, we launched this new movement with the Campaign Nonviolence Action Week, where 240 marches, rallies, demonstrations and interfaith services took place in every state across the nation. We followed this up with 370 events a year later. We have bolstered this by starting The Nonviolent Cities Project and the Thousand Nonviolence Trainings Project. People are taking hope from this vision.

Rivera Sun, Dariel Garner, Ryan Hall, Veronica Pelicaric, Kit Evans-Ford, Louie Vitale, and Sr. Janet Ryan — and a growing number of associates, promoters and action organizers – are Campaign Nonviolence's creative and powerful organizers and trainers. John Dear's decision to join Pace e Bene — which has facilitated over 800 nonviolence trainings, created numerous resources, including a series of books and study guides, and participated in and organized many movements and campaigns — has been a mutually transformative experience as he brings his experience and insight to the task of building a more nonviolent world.

As John says, "The days of violence are over." This is a stunning declaration. Can we end violence? In our lives? In our relationships? In our world? John's phrasing is both daunting and deeply hopeful, because if the days of violence are over, that means the days of definitive nonviolence are finally beginning.

This is, in spite of all the violence around us, what John is betting on.

And so are we.

25

Elizabeth Toyomi Okayama and Michael Yoshii: American History
August 9, 2012

It is late afternoon. The grounds are quiet and sun-drenched. The waters of Puget Sound lap against the nearby shoreline and a gentle summer breeze blows through. There is a restorative calm to the site, which makes the reality of what took place here seventy years ago all the more jarring.

On March 30, 1942, 227 children, women, and men of Japanese ancestry living on Bainbridge Island, Washington were taken from their homes, rounded up by soldiers armed with rifles fixed with bayonets, and herded onto the Eagledale Ferry Dock. After being transported to nearby Seattle they were sent by train to concentration camps in either Manzanar in California or Minidoka in Idaho. The Bainbridge Island contingent was the first group to be incarcerated under President Franklin Roosevelt's Executive Order 9066, which, following the Japanese attack on Pearl Harbor, authorized the military to exclude people of Japanese descent from much of the West Coast. Eventually 120,000 people were forced into 10 remote camps across the western U.S. until the end of World War II.

Like many of us, I was taught to call these sites "internment camps," a term designed to make a distinction between confinement and punishment, which sometimes refers to detaining belligerent armed forces, as spelled out in the Second Hague Convention. There is, however, a long history of referring to "a guarded compound for the detention or imprisonment of aliens, members of ethnic minorities, political opponents" as a "concentration camp," beginning as early as the 18th century in Poland. There is some evidence that FDR himself referred to the

U.S. sites as concentration camps. A vigorous discussion about the appropriate term has ensued for decades, with some commentators contesting the weakness and neutralizing concept of "internment." Without detracting from the horror experienced by others — including those who perished in the Nazi death camps — "concentration camp" conveys more accurately the chilling reality of what the Japanese American community faced.

A handful of us are touching this history this afternoon at the Bainbridge Island Japanese American Exclusion Memorial, a permanent site located near where the ferry landing once stood.

The heart of the site, which opened on August 6, 2011, is a low-slung, undulating 272-foot "Story Wall" evoking Japanese architectural forms that gently meanders down toward the water. The granite wall features the names and ages of Japanese Americans from the island who were forcibly incarcerated, as well as a series of images and quotations from a number of the involuntary exiles. As the memorial's website puts it, the wall tells "a unique American story of immigration, establishment, their forced removal and return to their island home."

This is a personal story for me. My mother-in-law, Elizabeth Toyomi Okayama, was a child in the camp at Heart Mountain in Wyoming. Like many others, her family was rounded up in Los Angeles and transported far from home. She arrived as a three-year-old and was freed when she was six. Her parents, fearing that they would face the kind of racism they experienced in California, opted for a new life in Chicago, where they opened restaurants and raised six children. Liz would later become a champion for justice—staffing an ecumenical women's center, co-writing an anti-racism curriculum, and working for decades with the Reconciling Ministries Network, a movement seeking, as its mission statement declares, to mobilize "United Methodists of all sexual orientations and gender identities to transform our Church and world into the full expression of Christ's inclusive love."

While Liz is not with me on this trip, my three-year-old daughter is, and it is poignantly bewildering to think of her being arrested, wrenched out of the world she knows, and held without due process for years.

Half of those incarcerated in this systematic sweep were children. The impact of this comes through in *The Children of the Camps*, a documentary that highlights the stories of six Japanese Americans who were interned as children and their exploration of the trauma of this experience of racism and scapegoating. The film features the work of Dr. Satsuki Ina, who was born in the Tule Lake concentration camp and who has developed a therapeutic approach focused on the process of telling personal stories.

Unearthing trauma in the midst of safe space can be transformative and healing. This is true in the classic therapeutic setting that Dr. Ina and others facilitate. But actively participating in nonviolent resistance injustice can also be transformative. Here, again, it is personal.

My wife, Cynthia Okayama Dopke, worked for several years at Buena Vista United Methodist Church, a predominantly Asian-American congregation in Alameda, California in the San Francisco Bay Area. Under the leadership of its pastor, Michael Yoshii, the church then – and now—incessantly works to translate its faith into practice by struggling for equality and dignity. He and the congregation advocate for the rights of immigrants, for justice for Palestine, and to end poverty. In the late 1990s when Cynthia was there, she and Michael organized a campaign that succeeded in getting a quarter of the housing stock on a local decommissioned naval base set aside as affordable housing for poor and low-income residents in the community.

Years before this, though, Yoshii was actively part of the movement to secure reparations for Japanese-Americans who had been forced into the World War II camps. His parents had been sent to camps; his mother in Arkansas, his father in Utah. In 1981, he testified before the Commission on Wartime Relocation and Internment of Civilians, that Congress had established—and was involved in the ongoing campaign that resulted in the Civil Liberties Act of 1988, which granted Japanese-Americans reparations— and an official government apology—to those who had been sent to the camps.

The experience of his family and the larger Japanese-American community during the Second World War has sharpened Yoshii's work for justice, including active vigilance and solidarity when other communities are at risk, including South Asian and Arab communities in the years since September 11, 2001. Like his work of connecting the dots, the film *Caught In Between* explicitly makes connections between 1942 and today's "war on terrorism" and its impact on U.S. Muslims, and the Heart Mountain Interpretive Center has featured an exhibit challenging stereotypes of Muslims.

The Bainbridge Island memorial exists as a bulwark against the corrosive effect of time and ideology that can calculatingly lull us into willful amnesia or diversionary ignorance. Even the silky, pastel light on this temperate summer day is unable to dull our awareness of the glaring meaning of this place.

Its motto — Nidoto Nai Yoni, "Let It Not Happen Again" — invites visitors to grapple with the realities of what occurred here and also, most pointedly, with how we can make good on this urgent command ringing across the decades.

This process of engagement is not only happening on Bainbridge Island. People are journeying to many of the camps, including Manzanar and Tule Lake in California. (Last month, the *New York Times* published an account of the journey 400 people recently made to the Tule Lake.) Pilgrimage to these and other such sites are acts of nonviolent transformation. They can change us and they can inspire us to change the world.

By their very presence, such sites relentlessly and publicly challenge the policies that spawned systemic violence and injustice, which gets me to think that we need such memorials everywhere, countering the historical and contemporary forms of exclusion, too often unseen and forgotten and thus continuing their originating trauma.

"Let It Not Happen Again" is applicable to many harrowing legacies — as today's grievous remembrance of the atomic bombing of Nagasaki reminds us — and so we are implored by history itself to remember and act in every possible way for the well-being of all.

26

Lennox Yearwood, Jr.: Forward Motion

February 7, 2013

Hip Hop Caucus is a national civil and human rights organization that mobilizes, educates and engages young people on "the social issues that directly impact their lives and communities." It has tenaciously set out to bridge racial, class and political divides by tackling police brutality, the disastrous federal response to Hurricane Katrina, the U.S. war in Iraq, youth violence and widespread, systematic attempts to prevent people of color from voting. It has been working on eco-justice and the climate crisis for years, including helping to organize the Green the Block campaign and the Green the City Summit.

Hip Hop Caucus' president, Rev. Lennox Yearwood, Jr., has been a tireless advocate for connecting the dots between poverty, racism, violence and environmental destruction — and for taking nonviolent action to create a more just, peaceful and sustainable world. For him, there are no silos separating social issues. I have seen this time and again over the last half-dozen years as we've worked together on numerous fronts, and also since he became a member of the board of Pace e Bene, a nonviolence training organization with whom I work.

I first met Rev. Yearwood — or, as he likes to be called, "Rev" — when he played an active role in the Declaration of Peace, a 2006 nationwide action campaign that called for a just and peaceful end to the U.S. war in Iraq. Although he had only founded Hip Hop Caucus two years earlier, Rev. Yearwood brought a wealth of experience to the table. In 2003 and 2004 he served as the Political and Grassroots Director of Russell Simmons' Hip Hop Summit Action Network and was also a key architect of P. Diddy's Citizen Change organization, known for its "Vote or Die!" campaign. He also worked on Jay-Z's Voice Your

Choice campaign and an AFL-CIO project called Hip Hop Voices. After Hurricane Katrina in 2005, Rev. Yearwood became the national director of the Gulf Coast Renewal Campaign, where he organized a coalition of national and grassroots organizations to advocate for the rights of Katrina survivors.

Partnering on the Declaration of Peace, I was struck by the deep passion Rev. Yearwood felt about ending the war. Though he was an officer and chaplain in the U.S. Air Force Reserve, he spoke out against the invasion of Iraq in 2003. As his outspoken anti-war resistance increased — including being arrested at the White House as part of the campaign to "declare peace" — the Air Force threatened him with a dishonorable discharge. When he resisted this step, the harassment escalated and he was threatened with deployment to Iraq, as well as a possible jail sentence.

In July 2007 he circulated a letter to U.S. peace and justice movements, explaining what was happening to him and asked for the support of U.S. citizens. The Air Force backed down after hearing from people across the country and around the world. "Thanks to my brothers and sisters in the movement," Yearwood wrote only a month after his appeal for support, "I will end my service with the honorable discharge that I earned. I am eternally grateful, and evermore committed to taking on the powers that be for the powers that ought to be." In 2007, he led the national "Make Hip Hop Not War" tour, linking the issues of the wars abroad with the violence in urban America.

Since then, Rev. Yearwood has kept at it on all fronts, linking injustice with the danger of the carbon crisis. In 2009, he and 350.org founder Bill McKibben co-wrote an op-ed titled "People, Let's Get Our Carbon Down" that — while publicizing the organization's first internationally-coordinated day of action that fall — emphasized the disproportionate impacts people of color and the poor face as a result of the climate crisis and environmental destruction. He recently joined McKibben in crisscrossing the country, sounding the climate crisis alarm.

When I caught up with him recently to ask him about his work for climate sanity, I found him as clear and committed as ever. "Justice," Rev. Yearwood told me, "is a tree with many branches, whether they are LGBT rights, or ending war, or ending torture or ending police brutality. This is one of the branches."

27
Medea Benjamin:
The Most Powerful Language
August 16, 2012 / May 27, 2016

CodePink founder Medea Benjamin and Franciscan Friar Louie Vitale had every intention of taking part in the recent Association for Unmanned Vehicle Systems International's North America trade show in Las Vegas, which amounted to a "drones convention" attended by thousands of people. Their aim was to talk with people, especially those staffing the 500 exhibits, to get more of an insider's perspective. Vitale has spent countless hours vigiling outside Creech Air Force Base north of Las Vegas, always with the hope of talking with the drone operators and their commanders. Even as he has been arrested a number of times at Creech for nonviolent civil disobedience, he's managed to engage in a dialogue occasionally with the personnel there. Now he wanted to hear from those who are promoting what seems to be a drones growth industry.

He didn't get the chance. Medea, who has a new book out about drones, and Vitale were singled out while in line and told that they were not allowed to attend, even though their $200 registration fee had been accepted beforehand.

"We know what you're up to," the security guard said, ushering them out of the building after they were threatened with arrest. They later joined a die-in outside the convention. A local newspaper columnist published a glowing piece on Vitale and Benjamin being pitched from the convention, while Benjamin in her own account asks:

> When are we, as a nation, going to have a frank discussion about drones and remote-controlled killing? One might

think that such a dialogue could take place when thousands of people come together, once a year, at the gathering of the Association of Unmanned Vehicle Systems International (AUVSI). Wrong.

As Vitale was taking part in the die-in, lying on the ground symbolizing the consequences of a drone attack as drone business was being transacted inside, he was overcome, he later said, with the emotional power of it all. It is this kind of experience that keeps him at the difficult but important work of making change. At 80, he has no plans to slow down.

Nor does Medea Benjamin. She's been at it for decades, crisscrossing the world for justice and peace, first with Global Exchange (which she co-founded in 1988) and then CodePink, a women-led force for good that tirelessly and creatively has organized countless campaigns and actions to, as the group says, end U.S. wars and militarism, support initiatives for peace and human rights initiatives, and invest our tax dollars in healthcare, education, green jobs and other life-affirming programs.

Like her action at the drones trade show, Benjamin leads by example—popping up in a Senate hearing room to call out a duplicitous policy-maker, making countless trips to Afghanistan, being arrested and deported protesting the house arrest of lawyers in Pakistan and demonstrating in Bahrain. In 2013, Benjamin interrupted a major speech by President Barack Obama on the War of Terror, delivered at the National Defense University. After she was removed from the room, the president said, "The voice of that woman is worth paying attention to," he said. "Obviously I do not agree with much of what she said. And obviously she wasn't listening to me and much of what I said. But these are tough issues. And the suggestion that we can gloss over them is wrong."

President Obama got it right—Medea Benjamin's voice is worth paying attention to. But even more than her words, it is how she delivers them that makes the difference. Nonviolent change hinges on provoking a long-term conversation with one's society, calling on it to see things it would rather not think about. The nonviolent change agent finds innumerable ways for society to pay attention and, gradually, change its mind.

There are many ways to do this, but none more compelling than using the most powerful language at our disposal: our own fragile, vulnerable and unarmed bodies. Medea Benjamin has been doing this for virtually her whole life, trespassing the circle of magical immunity that protects systems of violence and injustice—and being willing to face the consequences for doing so—so that all of us can, like her, see what's going on, and then do something about it.

28

Klaryta Antoszewska:
Nonviolent Lion for Justice

March 22, 2014

It's a striking image. At the culmination of a peace pilgrimage in 2007 from Las Vegas to the southern gate of the Nevada Test Site, Catholic Sister Klaryta Antoszewska crossed the line into the top-secret facility. Since 1982 thousands of people had done the same — first, to protest the detonation of 928 nuclear bombs since 1951, which ended with a U.S. moratorium on testing in the early 1990s, and more recently to urge the government to scrap its ongoing nuclear programs at the site and to return the land to the Western Shoshone nation. For the most part, the arrests over the years had been fairly choreographed, and the nonviolent protest that year, which included actor Martin Sheen, was no exception.

In a photo taken by an activist during the action, this Franciscan nun, like the others, is headed into the site — when she suddenly decides to grab onto the shirtsleeve of one of the Nye county officers. "Sr. Klaryta tries coaxing one of the sheriff's deputies across the line," reads the caption on the Nevada Desert Experience's website. Not having been there, I can't confirm that this is what she was doing, but if so, it was a potentially dangerous move. People had been tear-gassed in the past at the Nevada Test Site entrance, and she could have faced felony assault charges for simply touching a police officer, let alone yanking on his arm. But the photo shows her with a grin on her face, while the deputy — with his holstered handgun at the ready — seems both a bit surprised and playfully passive. He hasn't tensed and started into automatic reaction mode, even as she is moving gently but firmly forward, as if to say, "Come on, we have some work to do, ending the foolishness going on around here."

Sister Klaryta has died at the age of 81. She had been diagnosed with cancer last year and left Las Vegas where she had lived since 1976 for treatment in Southern California.

When I learned that she had passed away, I went searching online for the usual raft of sporadic obituaries — a practice that has become, in this virtual world of ours, a reflexive ritual of mourning and celebration, where we chance upon and savor the vestiges of a life strewn across the Internet. But when I searched for Klaryta, I turned up almost nothing. (The next day one obituary appeared.) This I take to be a clue to her life — and to the many Klarytas out there. She largely operated under the radar. Not being in the spotlight — or even leaving many virtual breadcrumbs — does not mean that she was not an agent for nonviolent change.

Indeed, despite her playful mien in the photograph, Klaryta was a lion for justice. While her work included decades of nonviolent resistance at the Nevada Test Site protesting nuclear arms, most of the time she grappled with the impact of the poverty and systemic dehumanization that those weapons systems help keep tightly in place. She worked with refugees — women, men and families from Guatemala and El Salvador, from Vietnam and China, from Russia and Latvia — as they tried to navigate the bewildering perils of Las Vegas where, like in most of the rest of America, it is a crime to be poor. She kept hordes of clothes and supplies of all kinds that she doled out relentlessly, kept the food coming, helped them find jobs. The lion came out when these human beings were pitilessly denied their humanity. When they were refused medical treatment, for example, she stormed into the hospital and wouldn't take no for an answer.

This fierce compassion didn't come out of thin air. Sr. Klaryta — born Ida Antoszewska — experienced the terror of war and institutionalized hatred as a girl in Poland during the Second World War. From what Klaryta indicated to those of us who knew her, her parents were part of the resistance to the Nazis who, among other things, smuggled food into the Jewish ghetto during the Holocaust. In the end, her mother was killed and her father was deported to Siberia. At 12 years old, as the oldest of three children, she became the head of the household.

After the war she became a member of the Sisters of St. Francis of Penance and Christian Charity in Orlik, Poland, taking the name Klaryta. Was there something in Saint Francis' story that spoke to her own — the medieval saint whose journey to religious life was inextricably bound to his experience of war (the horror of medieval combat, followed by a year as a prisoner of war) that led him to an unquenchable thirst for peacemaking and the well-being of all?

Klaryta's experience of unspeakable violence led her to a lifelong journey to mend the utter brokenness of the world, especially as it seeks to systematically crush the most expendable. This determination worked itself out in resisting the violence of poverty as well as the violence of the nuclear threat. It is her history, and the history of all others who have been caught in the suffocating cage of war and structural violence, that she brought to the gates of a nuclear test site, hoping to contribute, in some small way, to freeing those on all sides of that line.

Sr. Klaryta studied theology, languages and philology. One of her teachers, Karol Józef Wojtyła, would later become Pope John Paul II. In the 1960s, she was sent to Rome, where she worked at the Vatican in the Office of Peace and Justice. In 1976 she accompanied Sister Rosemary Lynch, of the same religious community, to Las Vegas, where they established the Sisters of Saint Francis Social and Refugee Program. It was here that Sister Rosemary would wander out to the desert adjoining the 1,350 square mile nuclear test site to pray for an end to the nuclear blasts that, on average, took place every 18 days there. Eventually Sr. Klaryta joined her there as a new anti-nuclear movement took shape.

Julia Occhiogrosso, the founder of the Las Vegas Catholic Worker who knew Sr. Klaryta for many years, recalls how Sr. Klaryta took few pains to mask the anger she felt at injustice. Eventually, Julia came to see this flinty, angry glare for what it likely was — a profound anxiety rooted in the experience of the horrendous violence she had experienced. These experiences did not destroy her. In fact, she channeled her deep response to them for healing those who, like her, had in many cases faced enormous violence and were now trying to fashion a new life.

Sr. Klaryta was not alone in being unsung. There are many unrecognized agents of nonviolent transformation keeping the world from flying apart — and preparing the ground for the nonviolent shift that the survival of the planet and its inhabitants requires. She, like many who are methodically but quietly building a better world, are saying with their actions and sometimes with their words, "Come on, we have some work to do, ending the foolishness going on around here."

29

Jack Healey: Human Rights Impresario
March 8, 2012

Changing the world for good doesn't depend on money, status, or political power. It hinges, instead, on ordinary people unleashing their creativity and gumption.

This is not an airy theory for Jack Healey. It's something he has experienced throughout his life. The former executive director of Amnesty International USA took another opportunity to spread this news recently when he spoke to a group of college students in Chicago.

His message to them: Shake off any powerlessness that might be holding you back from making a difference. At a time when the concern for human rights has been largely sidelined in the national conversation, tap your power to work for those rights in their most comprehensive sense: from jobs to justice. In short, take action for a world where everyone matters.

Healey's presentation was, though, more than pithy marching orders. It was a stream of stories—weighty, startling, profound, and occasionally humorous—which, drawn from his fifty years as an agent for change, made the point repeatedly that people power works.

Healey is most famous for pioneering rock activism. When he came to Amnesty in 1981, he envisioned increasing the organization's membership; building its capacity to respond to human rights violations worldwide; and contributing to mainstreaming the notion of human rights. He decided to do this through music.

In the 1980s and 1990s Healey brought some of the world's biggest rock stars together to tour for human rights, including Sting, U2, Bruce Springsteen, Youssou N'dour, Tracy Chapman, and Peter Gabriel. On the 40th anniversary of the Universal

Declaration of Human Rights, for example, he organized "Human Rights Now," a tour featuring concerts in 20 cities across the planet, including New Delhi, Harare, Abidjan, São Paulo, Buenos Aires, Budapest, Montreal, Barcelona, and Tokyo. This initiative highlighted massive human rights violations and brought a message of hope and empowerment. It was an historic outpouring of music for social change experienced by a million people on nearly every continent.

Born in 1938 in Pittsburgh into a large Irish family of coal miners and steel mill workers, Healey became involved in the Civil Rights Movement during the 1960s as a theology student in Washington, D.C. During that period, he attended a talk by Dorothy Day, co-founder of the Catholic Worker movement who, he now says, had a pivotal impact on him. So did a comment by theologian Rabbi Abraham Heschel, who said that the key to wisdom was curiosity. Healey remembers saying to himself at the time, "I'm going to be curious, because I want to get some of that wisdom!"

Jack's curiosity led him all over the world. Ordained a Catholic priest in 1966, Healey directed a campus ministry center in Maryland. After leaving the priesthood in 1968, he organized walk-a-thons throughout the U.S. in which hundreds of thousands of young people raised millions of dollars for the fight against world hunger; worked with comedian and activist Dick Gregory; and served as director of the Peace Corps in southern Africa for five years. These experiences prepared him for his twelve-year tenure at Amnesty, where he led the organization into an era of unprecedented growth and effectiveness. Under his leadership, Amnesty strengthened its ability to address torture, the death penalty, political imprisonment, and other human rights abuses.

Healey left Amnesty in 1993. He now directs the Human Rights Action Center in Washington, D.C., where he continues to campaign for justice and human dignity.

In 1999 Healey traveled to Rangoon to meet with Aung San Suu Kyi, the Nobel Peace Prize winner whose party, the National League for Democracy, had decisively won the 1990 national election in Burma. In response, she was placed under house arrest by the military, where she remained for 15 out of the next 21 years, until her most recent release in November 2010. After their 1999 meeting, he returned to the U.S. committed to help free her and to support the pro-democracy movement in Burma. He organized a variety of projects, including concerts, a compact disk, and thirty online videos to help raise the visibility of her case and the struggle in Burma. He also played a key role in the U.S. Campaign for Burma.

These days he continues to work on a long-term project to raise the visibility of the Universal Declaration of Human Rights, including a campaign to have it printed in every passport. Having these rights written down and widely recognized, he stresses, can be the basis of innumerable movements for change.

For as long as I've known Jack Healey, I've seen that this is how his mind works. He possesses a comprehensive vision of a more just and nonviolent world, but he doesn't tarry much with the abstract ideal. (As he said to the students, "We know injustice when we see it. Justice is another matter.") Instead, he is endlessly devising creative maneuvers designed to mess with the current cultural arrangements and to prod us to think concretely about fixing what's broken—and then getting to it.

PART THREE:

Nonviolent Lives Working Together

We have to make truth and nonviolence not matters for mere individual practice but for practice by groups and communities and nations. That at any rate is my dream. I shall live and die in trying to realize it.

— Mohandas Gandhi

History is made by people. Not by mysterious collective forces or abstract social causes. Specific flesh-and-blood human beings, all of us, continually act — individually and collectively, intentionally and unintentionally — to construct and reconstruct our societies and cultures. In doing so, we become the creators of the social worlds we inhabit and co-authors of the social story we call history.

— Christian Smith

Living as we are in a time of emergency, thrown together in companionship with others of different races and creeds, let us try to think of ourselves as a community. Let us live in peace, and then we are a little oasis of peace in a war-torn world. Let us have no bitterness, no class strife, so that we can build up our strength to work for justice and love. Let us pray together, no matter what our faith is, for each other and for the whole world.

— Dorothy Day

Social movements have played a central role throughout history in achieving positive social change. Rooted in grassroots "people power," nonviolent social movements have been a powerful means for ordinary people to act on their deepest values and to successfully challenge immoral and unjust social conditions and policies, despite the determined resistance of entrenched powerholders.

— Bill Moyer

30
The American Revolution:
A Nonviolent Beginning
July 4, 2013

After a peripatetic life careening around Europe in the mid-19th century, a penniless Karl Marx spent long years at a desk in the British Museum writing *Das Kapital*, a work that laid out the economic laws of capitalist society — and would go on to have a vast impact globally through most of the following century.

What would the history of the past hundred years have been like had the Marxian engine toward the classless society been nonviolent people power rather than violent class struggle? What if a character more like Gandhi had staked out that desk in London — fresh, perhaps, from the movement that successfully ended British slavery — and churned out a text offering a diagnosis every bit as apt as Marx's (perhaps not unlike the Mahatma's own analysis of global capital in his still-useful 1909 tome, *Hind Swaraj*, or *Indian Self-Rule*), but with a radically different method for proceeding?

History, though, is what actually occurred — not what we hope occurred. On one level there is little more than entertainment value in spinning out intriguing and untethered counter-histories, the way a certain literary cottage industry does. (What if the South had won the Civil War? What if Albert Einstein had never lived? What if Israel had been temporarily established in Alaska after World War II and not in the Middle East?)

On another level, though, this kind of speculation might get us to wonder about what is being written now — and its potential consequences. Is there, for example, a Gandhian Marx somewhere, perhaps in exile and penury, dutifully plodding away at the *Nonviolent Das Kapital* — a book that will breathlessly capture the imagination of people across the planet and go on to function as a template for the operating systems of whole societies in the next generation, or the next century?

We haven't seen this definitive text yet. Maybe we never will. Perhaps something like Marx's book was so unique that it proved to be a historical one-off, so that even *considering* this possibility is a time-wasting detour. Or maybe books have had their day, and something else is going to come along to take their place.

If, however, this decisive volume does spring itself on humanity, it may be because the ground has been laid. First: the gathering momentum of nonviolent people power movements around the globe has nudged even the most skeptical observers to somehow take notice. It is the experience of public and engaged nonviolence, especially over the past half century, that has prompted concerted attention, just as the experience of violent revolution in Marx's day prompted sociological focus. Second: an increasingly powerful lineage of nonviolence research and analysis has created a growing stream of books that have gone a long way in establishing not only a discipline but a genre. From Gene Sharp's 1973 ground-breaking three-volume *The Politics of Nonviolent Action* forward, we are living in a time of immense data-collection and writing on the dynamics, methods and history of nonviolent change.

A powerful addition to this growing bibliography is *Recovering Nonviolent History: Civil Resistance in Liberation Struggles*, a new collection edited by Maciej J. Bartkowski. Here the authors ask a powerful question of the historical experience of national or societal liberation: has nonviolent civil resistance played an often ignored or forgotten role in these efforts? In the 15 cases featured here that represent almost every continent — from Ghana and Mozambique to Algeria and Iran, from Burma and Bangladesh to Hungary and Kosovo — the answer is a resounding, "Yes."

In every case, scholars burrow into the experience of each society — generally over a time-frame of decades or even centuries

— and identify often forgotten or repressed nonviolent movements that displayed a wide repertoire of tactics and which typically enlisted people from across society. These campaigns have often been central to the creation of parallel institutions, traditions and practices of civil society, and frameworks for participatory post-conflict societies. In fact, one of this book's key contributions is its focus on how nonviolent strategies have been central to the identity formation of emergent societies and nations both during and after liberation struggles.

In some of the cases studied here, nonviolent campaigns have existed alongside armed struggle. Often, the memory of civil resistance has been obscured or even suppressed for a variety of ideological reasons (by regimes who consider violent combat more patriotic or whose own violent strategies are legitimated by a violent origin) or scholarly methodological biases. By focusing on nonviolent civil resistance, the book's contributors illuminate an often forgotten history, but also demonstrate how key these efforts were to successful liberation movements.

Two sections of the book are of particular note. The chapter on Egypt sheds light on the historical roots of Egypt's pro-democracy struggle since the Arab Spring of 2011. And the chapter on the birth of the United States throws into new relief our annual celebration of Independence Day.

The section on Egypt is a detailed reading of the history of nonviolent people power. Amr Abdalla and Yasmine Arafa's chapter analyzes the country's nonviolent resistance against foreign occupation, including the 1805 revolution's street demonstrations, civil disobedience and a nonviolent siege; the 1881 movement sparked by Colonel Ahmed Orabi that won short-term demands and laid the groundwork for future mass-based campaigns; nonviolent resistance to British rule; and the 1919 revolution that led to formal independence in 1922, that included gathering 100,000 signatures on a prohibited petition, public statements, student demonstrations and strikes, workers' and peasants' strikes, public participation of women, demonstrations at public funerals, mass prayer and other forms of resistance. This essay documents a consistent spirit of nonviolent action, as echoed in Orabi's statement about the 1881 movement: "Whoever has read history knows that European countries earned their freedom by violence, bloodshed and destruction, but we earned it in one hour without shedding a drop of blood, without putting fear in a heart, without transgressing on someone's right, or damaging someone's honor."

Walter H. Conser, Jr.'s chapter on the U.S. struggle for independence opens with President John Adams' assertion in an 1815 letter that "a history of military operations... is not a history of the American Revolution. The revolution was in the hearts and minds of the people, and in the union of the colonies; both of which were substantially effected before hostilities commenced."

This nonviolent revolution took place between 1765 and 1775, marked by the campaigns against the Stamp Act and the Townshend Acts and the establishment of the Committees of Correspondence. This decade of nonviolent action included open resistance to specific acts of the British government, mass political and economic non-cooperation with British authority, and the development of parallel institutions, including institutions of government. Like Gandhi, the American colonists organized an obstructive program (denying the British the fruits of occupation through non-importation, non-consumption, and non-exportation) and a constructive program (creating new political institutions, like the First Continental Congress). "Self-government in the colonies was not gained by the war, as is so often assumed," Conser writes. "It was actually established much earlier."

If the nonviolent strategy was successful, why did the Americans resort to military operations in late 1775? Conser's answer is that the colonists "underestimated or misunderstood the gains that the nonviolent resistance had achieved" and that the Second Continental Congress recruited European allies who drew on their experience to craft a military strategy. The same Congress proceeded to form an army.

While Conser judges this as a shift in strategy, Jonathan Schell in his book *The Unconquerable World: Power, Nonviolence and the Will of the People*, frames it slightly differently. Schell, also working from letters by John Adams, asserts like Conser that the revolution was nonviolent. Once it was won, Schell says, the newly sovereign United States moved to defend itself militarily from "a foreign power seeking to force the new country back into its empire." Schell quotes Adams as he takes umbrage at long-retired generals conflating the two in their memoirs. When Adams learns that Congress has hired a national painter, he argues that the paintings should be scenes of protest.

History is what actually occurred. But what if what actually occurred turns out to be different than we thought? What if what sounds like literary counter-history turns out to be true? Maybe the great, definitive, earth-shaking tome of nonviolence that we are anticipating is actually history itself, waiting to be parsed with finer and finer precision and surprise.

The United States may have turned out differently if its nonviolent origins had been taught, acknowledged and taken to heart over the past two centuries. But there's no time like the present. Thanks to *Recovering Nonviolent History* and *The Unconquerable World*, it's not too late to celebrate — and draw the beckoning conclusions from — the Nonviolent Fourth of July.

31

The Great LGBTQ March:
"We Are Everywhere"
October 11, 2012

In October 1979, the lesbian, gay, bisexual, transgender and queer community mounted the first National March on Washington for Lesbian and Gay Rights. An estimated 75,000 to 125,000 marchers descended on the nation's capital to demand equal rights and to call for the passage of civil rights legislation. As historian Amin Ghaziani has written, this was "the symbolic coming out and birth of a national movement for lesbian and gay rights." In addition to signaling the emergence of this social and political force, the march overcame widespread isolation within the movement itself by "linking local lesbian and gay communities in a highly symbolic, concentrated physical space."

In the years that followed, the need was less to inaugurate the movement than to challenge the institutionalized homophobia of the Reagan administration and demand a concerted national response to the AIDS crisis. On October 11, 1987 — 25 years ago today — a new wave of marchers flooded into Washington to make their case for change as part of the second National March on Washington for Lesbian and Gay Rights. Organizers put the number of participants at between 500,000 and 650,000. There would be other national marches for LGBTQ rights after this one, but this event — because of its size, scope and success — has often been dubbed "The Great March." October 11 is now National Coming Out Day, which was established in 1988 to commemorate the 1987 march.

I was fortunate to be there that day. I had arrived in Washington a few weeks before to begin a new job as the national co-coordinator of the Pledge of Resistance, a nationwide, nonviolent direct action network working to end the U.S. wars in Central America. I would soon find out that demonstrations take place in the nation's capital virtually every day — but this was different. For many of us this was the largest crush of humanity we will likely ever experience. As the march lunged its way around the newly created AIDS Memorial Quilt with its 1920 panels carpeting part of the National Mall, we became an enormous throng roiling methodically toward the stage in the shadow of the U.S. Capitol. No matter where we stood, there seemed to be no beginning and no end. It was as if, drawn from every part of this nation, this vast ad hoc community was slowly inching its way from the margins to the center, propelled by forces of history that none of us controlled but were moving with a power — composed, disciplined and relentless — to which each of us made a small, incremental contribution.

An impromptu chant rolled through this sea of humanity: *We are everywhere*. It was a sonorous round, bending and rising, spreading out in every direction — a refrain that became the soundtrack for this august pilgrimage of power and potential. One voice composed of many voices rang out — voices from every part of this land, voices from the suppressed past and the unknowable future, intoning with richness and authority an unshakable truth: *LGBTQ people are everywhere*.

This somber but also bracing spectacle was profoundly transformative. I felt something loosen within and peel away. Something of my own hetero-centric socialization, the homophobic training I had been put through subtly and not so subtly in my life, that I had uncritically accepted and taken in. At its very best, ritual works a subtle magic — and it was working.

It dawned on me that it was a precious gift to walk side by side with those who had been on this arduous pilgrimage their whole lives. It was a gift to be present, to be with hundreds of thousands of human beings who carried the woundedness of living in a systemically homophobic culture, but who also bore in their own flesh the sacredness of survival and the luminous intimations of resilience and infinite worth. To be together in this highly symbolic and concentrated (but also potentially healing and freeing) space was an inestimable, unmerited grace.

But the transformational energy did not end there.

Two days later 800 people trooped over to the doorways and lawns of the U.S. Supreme Court to protest its 1986 decision upholding sodomy laws in *Bowers v. Hardwick*. Thus positioned, they refused to leave. I spent the morning watching civilly disobedient groups of five or ten people at a time being plucked from the grounds of the court and taken off under arrest to be booked and dealt with. The initial opening of the heart I had experienced on the march now dramatically expanded. Seeing one human being after another willingly risk arrest and face the consequences that it might entail reached my core. I felt my own mind and soul irrevocably transformed.

Even though I had been practicing civil disobedience for some years by then, it was a revelation seeing the arrests at the U.S. Supreme Court that day. I understood in a new way how the voluntary willingness to put one's body potentially in harm's way for justice — especially when this is done by those who have faced the brunt of injustice their whole lives — can speak powerfully and deeply to the right brain of onlookers and, under the proper conditions, of a whole society. It is extraordinarily unfair that the very people who are most violated by the world are often the ones who are most called to assume the burden of transforming it, but it seems to be one of the laws of the universe. While there were allies among the arrested that day, it was mostly people who had experienced the structural violence of politically-and culturally-enforced homophobia who made the decision to face the consequences for nonviolently disrupting the machinery of that oppression using the most powerful symbol at their disposal: their own vulnerable bodies.

One of the allies who help lead the 1987 march was César Chávez, the co-founder of the United Farm Workers who had a long history of supporting the LGBTQ movement, and who understood the power of nonviolent action to change hearts and to change society. As Ian Stokell and Steve Lee reported earlier this year:

> Chávez was the first major civil rights leader to support gay and lesbian issues visibly and explicitly. He spoke out on behalf of lesbian, gay, bisexual and transgender people in the 1970s. "César Chávez did not only speak at our 1987 March on Washington but walked the entire march route. His granddaughter Christine Chávez told me that it was the biggest crowd he ever spoke to," said former National Gay and Lesbian Task Force board member and San Diego city commissioner, Nicole Murray Ramirez. "He never forgot the support the UFW received from the gay community."

This is just another reason to celebrate the Obama administration's decision to designate Chávez's home in California's Tehachapi Mountains a national monument this week.

Movements seeking justice have been organizing marches to Washington at least since 1894 when Jacob Coxey led "Coxey's Army" of 500 of the unemployed on a trek from Ohio to the nation's capital during the second year of a four-year depression to urge the government to create a jobs program. Instead of employment opportunities they were confronted by 1,500 troops, with Coxey and others arrested for walking on the Capitol lawn. (Some scholars think that Coxey's march may have inspired "The Wizard of Oz," whose author, Frank Baum, witnessed the march.)

Since then over 100 marches in Washington of varying sizes and from across the political spectrum have been organized. Some of them, like the Civil Rights movement's 1963 March on

Washington, have achieved indelible historic status because they clearly and dramatically laid a compelling choice before the country: *Will we take our nation's values seriously or not?* The 1987 National March for Lesbian and Gay Rights takes its place alongside these iconic pilgrimages for justice, not only because it responded forcefully to the dramatic challenges at that critical moment, but because it fueled the many difficult but powerful struggles and accomplishments of the movement over the past few decades.

32

The Pilgrimage to Montgomery:
Then and Now

March 22, 2012

On March 21, 1965 Martin Luther King Jr. set out with 3,200 civil rights activists from Selma to Montgomery, the capital of Alabama, to call on the state and the nation to dismantle the structural obstacles to suffrage for African Americans. Two weeks before, on Sunday, March 7, hundreds of marchers had been brutally attacked on the Edmund Pettus Bridge by Alabama state troopers and local police officers on horses wielding clubs and whips amid a storm of tear gas.

"Bloody Sunday" horrified the nation and motivated a reluctant Lyndon Johnson to provide federalized National Guard protection for a renewed march, after the movement succeeded in getting a court order to allow the demonstrators to proceed. As federal judge Frank M. Johnson Jr. ruled, "The law is clear that the right to petition one's government for the redress of grievances may be exercised in large groups ... and these rights may be exercised by marching, even along public highways." Over the next four days, the marchers walked 50 miles, sleeping at night in fields alongside Jefferson Davis Highway. Over 25,000 people arrived at Alabama's Capitol building on March 25. Less than five months later, Johnson signed the Voting Rights Act of 1965 into law.

Though this watershed moment took place nearly five decades ago, its power remains undiminished. For years this event has been marked with gatherings, speeches and reenactments of this now-archetypal journey for justice. Nonviolent change is often a journey that is new and uncharted—breaking new ground, setting a new direction; at the same time, its power can also derive from retracing and giving new meaning to a past path for freedom. It can be improvisational and creative. And it can be rooted in acts of remembrance and reenactment. A word that works for both of these realities is "pilgrimage."

This year, the League of United Latin American Citizens (LULAC), the Hispanic Council and the Labor Council for Latin American Advancement (LCLAA) joined with countless other civil rights organizations in the Selma-to-Montgomery march as an opportunity to take a stand against Alabama's anti-Latino legislation, HB 56, considered the strictest anti-immigrant bill passed by any state in the U.S. The president of the Leadership Conference on Civil and Human Rights, Wade Henderson, wrote:

> The recent 47th commemoration of the Bloody Sunday March of 1965 marks a new phase in the civil rights movement. It represents a turning point for people from all backgrounds, who are joining together, not only to remember our shared past, but also to fight for a shared future. It's a moment of recognition from all sides that, though our nation has progressed since 1965, we are not yet finished with the struggle to include everyone in the fullness that American life has to offer.

For Henderson, the past and the present are colliding, and just as people took action half a century ago, it is critically important to draw on that same energy and example to continue to struggle: "The state of Alabama ... is once again using fear and intimidation as weapons against those without power. This time, the targets are Latinos and the aim is to drive them from their homes and their communities."

The original Selma-to-Montgomery march was not a choreographed or historically enshrined ritual. It was a radically ad hoc set of strategies that had to be revised over and over again until, improbably, the waters parted. Improvised as it was—

playing each new factor by ear—the journey nonetheless was a pilgrimage: "a sacred journey" or "a journey of transformation."

At the same time, this ongoing pilgrimage deepens the march's original meaning by using its memory on behalf of unfinished business. Like many geographical nodes of the civil rights itinerary spread across the South and beyond, Selma is a destination that joins past and present in new and creative ways. The route to the capital is even memorialized as the Selma-to-Montgomery Voting Rights Trail, a U.S. National Historic Trail.

The anthropologist James Preston speaks of pilgrimage as "spiritual magnetism." Theologian Richard R. Niebuhr writes that pilgrims "are persons in motion—passing through territories not their own—seeking something we might call completion." For me, pilgrimage is a journey to the depths of reality, including its woundedness and sacredness, seeking the power and possibility of healing and transformation.

Pilgrimage, in this sense, is not simply a solo act—it is not simply a quest for individual fulfillment. It is a process of engaging the reality of injustice and violence as well as the potential for nonviolent change, and even reconciliation.

This is why I have a keen interest in the many forms of social change that literally involve *movement*, including Gandhi's Salt March, the United Farm Workers' 1966 march to Sacramento, the decades of nonviolent civil disobedience at the Nevada Test Site (which requires a journey into the simultaneously empty and rich Nevada desert), or innumerable marches organized by the peace, environmental, labor and Occupy movements.

Marches, walks and processions are not simply a way to "be visible"; they are symbolic journeys from A (the grinding present) to B (a more just and peaceful world). They are dramatized expeditions to a center of significance. They seek a metamorphosis of conditions. And they deliver the message in person. Such journeys accrue their meaning by taking each step, by sleeping by the side of the road, by gauging the tremendous dangers and possible opportunities of doing so. No doubt the Southern Christian Leadership Conference or its allies could have rented a fleet of buses to make the trip from Selma to Montgomery in about an hour. The meaning of the experience, though, included the totality of the journey. Without this tremendously symbolic and tremendously physical dimension, the exercise may well have been pointless.

In 1995, on the 30th anniversary of Selma, then-former Governor George Wallace attended the commemoration. The one who had once staked his political career and national reputation on such inflammatory racist rhetoric as "Segregation then, segregation now, segregation forever," held hands with African-Americans and sang "We Shall Overcome." Colman McCarthy describes the scene:

> It was a reaching-out moment of reconciliation, of Wallace's asking for—and receiving—forgiveness. In a statement read for him—he was too ill to speak—Wallace told those in the crowd who had marched 30 years ago: "Much has transpired since those days. A great deal has been lost and a great deal gained, and here we are. My message to you today is, welcome to Montgomery. May your message be heard. May your lessons never be forgotten." In gracious and spiritual words, Joseph Lowery, a leader in the original march and now the president of the Southern Christian Leadership Conference, thanked the former separatist "for coming out of your sickness to meet us. You are a different George Wallace today. We both serve a God who can make the desert bloom. We ask God's blessing on you."

In reflecting on this exchange, McCarthy was reminded of what Dr. King had once said:

"Forgiveness does not mean ignoring what has been done or putting a false label on an evil act. It means, rather, that the evil act no longer remains as a barrier to the relationship. ... While abhorring segregation, we shall love the segregationist. This is the only way to create the beloved community."

Dr. King wrote an autobiographical essay entitled "Pilgrimage to Nonviolence." As it did for him, the pilgrimage metaphor can capture for us the struggles of the journey. But it can also hold out the possibility of arriving at the spiritual center, what he deemed "the beloved community." Such a move can, if only for a moment, reward those longings that have propelled us forward, including the desire to experience a transforming kind of power, to discover a new reality, to answer an inner call, to reclaim our true selves, to seek pardon—and even to experience a miracle.

33

A New Chicago Peace Movement: "What Do We Want...?"

June 28, 2013

By the time I arrived at St. Sabina Church on Chicago's South Side on the first day of summer, 500 people had already crowded into the street at the side of the 80-year-old building, waving signs and engrossed in a smattering of speeches from the makeshift podium. A smothering thunderstorm had rocked the city only hours before, but by now the roiling clouds had given way to a clear, pastel sky.

Those who gathered had another storm on their minds: the tornados of gun violence that regularly tear through this neighborhood, Auburn Gresham, and many others across the city, including Englewood, Lawndale, Pilsen, Back of the Yards, Austin. The previous weekend, 46 people had been shot in Chicago, including seven homicides, and already that afternoon a 31-year-old man had been slain.

In recent years summer on Chicago's south and west sides has come to be associated less with vacations and leisure than with the annual upsurge in gang violence. Many of the participants had recently lost loved ones to such violence, and were resolved to stand against this trauma that irreparably tears through lives, families and whole communities. The mood was mournful but also defiant.

A peace movement is gaining traction here. It is not protesting a foreign war. It is not trying to catch the ear of the president. Instead, it is trained on the community. Like all peace movements, this one is going public to challenge the presumed inevitability of war, to break its inexorable spell, and to open psychological space for an alternative. All movements contest the

160

dominant narratives, especially those that stubbornly feed the paralyzing assumption that there is nothing that can be done. This is what the rally and march last Friday night was about, beginning with its theme, "Occupy the Streets."

The organizers have taken on the central metaphor of the recent Occupy movement, but have expanded it dramatically. This movement is not about staying put on a specific plot of real estate. Instead, "occupy" here means a process whereby the entirety of the neighborhood — and, ultimately, the city — is engaged, revitalized and transformed.

Fr. Michael Pfleger — St. Sabina's pastor who has been actively challenging the violence, and the poverty and racism that spawns it, for decades — put it this way at the opening rally: "We cannot wait for law enforcement or for government. We must run our homes. We must run our neighborhoods. We must occupy the streets. We must come out of our houses, out of our churches, out of our businesses, and be the presence in our communities." He continued, "We must be the eyes and ears of the community — to let our children know that we are watching over you and we will protect you. *We* are 911. *We* are the blue lights. We're the Interrupters. *We* are in charge of the community... Occupy the streets. We must reach out to our brothers in the community. Stop demonizing them! Stop telling them they are nothing but gang bangers. Let them know you're our sons, you're our daughters, we love you and respect you. But we also want to send a clear message: We have zero tolerance for shooting or killing."

For Fr. Pfleger, these words are not only rousing oratory. They are a call to action backed up with a thoroughgoing plan. He is serious about challenging the cycles of violence that are reinforced, from his perspective, by inaction by the rest of the community. That's why "Occupy the Streets" will be marching every Friday night throughout the summer. Like last week's march, they will repeatedly trespass the "us vs. them" arrangements that all but guarantee sprees of escalatory violence.

They, like the marchers that assembled last week, will walk through multiple gang territories.

But this summer-long action campaign will not be restricted to public witness. It is a 24/7 job that everyone can take up. "Our message is clear," Pfleger said with steely urgency. "Chicago, this summer, get out of your homes. Get out of your churches. Get out of your synagogues. Get out of your mosques. Get out from behind closed doors and blinds. Break the code of silence and apathy. Be the boots on the ground on your block. You may not be able to change a city. But guess what? You can change your block. You can change your house. You can change where you live... Let's occupy the streets. Let's march. Let's let our children know we've got their back."

For years, Pfleger and Saint Sabina Church have been engaged in the kind of up-close conflict transformation he's urging all of us to take up and multiply. A recent example is a project the church started last September: a 16-week basketball tournament in which teams are formed with members from different gangs. Not only do they play together, they also eat together and attend conflict resolution sessions together.

There have been some perks — including tickets to Chicago Bulls games doled out by some of the team's players, with the proviso that members of different gangs sit together in the luxury boxes provided by the NBA team. Two tournaments have been held so far, and the plan seems to be paying off. Since September there have only been two violent episodes in the neighborhood, and neither was perpetrated by the gangs involved in the basketball program. This is only one of the many programs that the church has built to grapple with the violence that flows from the structural violence of racism and economic injustice.

After a haunting rendition of the Sam Cooke classic "A Change is Gonna Come" sung by a young man in the community who had recently competed in NBC's reality show *The Voice*, the march stepped off. People of all ages floated out into a normally busy 79th Street — it had been shut down by the police — with a pensive urgency, waving signs that read "Stop Killing Our Future" and "Guns Are for Cowards." In keeping with the evening's theme, signs in English and Spanish scattered across the march commanded us to "Occupy the Streets with Peace." The words, for this moment, were translated into reality.

The resolve in the gait of the marchers seemed to dramatize the fact that what appeared to be a typical march was, in fact, a journey of life and death. This was a relentless journey through a terrain where life and death all too needlessly trade places — but also a journey toward another outcome. A profoundly rooted longing for a nonviolent alternative seemed to pervade the crowd — a longing that appeared to deepen as we walked the narrower streets lined with houses and children streamed out of the night to join in, with their parents in tow. These two- and three-year olds now seemed determined to lead the section of the march I found myself in, energetically scrambling ahead of us as if lunging toward some finish line — as if straining toward a future with some substantial chance to live and even flourish.

Then I heard it. The low rumble of a chant washed over us from the unseen front of the march. Though I have heard it for many years in many other marches, when the chant reached us I realized that it was like hearing it for the very first time:

What do we want?

Peace!

When do we want it?

Now!

What do we want? The lines were big and bold and urgent. *Peace! Now!* The questions and answers ricocheted down the line,

163

bouncing off the nearby buildings and homes, saturated with a poignancy and resonance where death and injuries from gun violence — this week, this *day* — is skyrocketing. This was not a peace for some far off place. It was a peace that needed to happen, to come alive, to occupy this place.

Here. Now.

Friday night's pilgrimage set off into the unknown to fill the streets with peace, even as the first weekend of the summer saw another turn in the deadly wheel of violence. They will continue this work week after week this summer, undaunted in their resolve to build a powerful and transformative peace movement at home.

34

Not in Our Town: Upending the Script
November 3, 2011

The scripts run deep. Faced with violence or injustice, we've often been trained by our families, our media, and our societies to react in one of three basic ways: avoidance, accommodation or violence. These well-grooved neural pathways are not only moral positions—they are often survival strategies. Not getting involved, going along or meeting violence with violence promises us survival and safety.

These scripts, though, often upend this promise by failing to engage deeply and effectively with the realities at hand. The conflicts in our lives or our world have a life of their own, feeding and stoking the embers of fear, powerlessness, despair and retaliation if they're not dealt with. Often it's only a matter of time before another fire gets rolling.

In spite of the tenacity of these scripts, a nonviolent shift is underway. This doesn't mean a utopia free of violence and injustice is coming. Instead, it means we are steadily creating resources and practices that equip more and more people to deal effectively with the violence they face. This transition, in fact, also includes a shift of thinking for those of us who are peacemakers: from a vision of establishing an impossibly idealistic world to one where, while still facing violence and injustice, tools for nonviolent transformation are more plentiful, accessible, and increasingly the default.

We are living in a time when these resources for nonviolent change are proliferating, from restorative justice to trauma healing; from nonviolent communication to forgiveness research; from anti-racism training to third-party nonviolent intervention. Each of these "transformation technologies" offers options beyond the deeply ingrained scripts.

One such practice that has emerged over the past fifteen years is the Not In Our Town movement.

Unlike the exclusivism of its NIMBY cousin (working to keep everything from homeless shelters to toxic waste plants out of its "backyard"), the Not In Our Town movement is not about protecting its existing milieu as much as coming to grips with that milieu's violence and doing something about it.

A hate crime occurs every hour in the U.S., and the Not In Our Town movement has produced a series of powerful documentaries since 1994 (many broadcast on public television) that highlight ways that cities, towns, and schools have grappled with hate crimes in an active healing, and effective way.

A project of The Working Group, NIOT's first video focused on Billings, Montana, where members of the Jewish community were under attack by hate groups in the early 1990s. Rather than avoiding or accommodating these episodes, town-members publicly demonstrated their solidarity with their besieged neighbors. Since then, the series has focused on a wide spectrum of hate crimes.

The Working Group's goal is not simply to document and disseminate a series of moving stories, but to support and help build a movement that challenges hate from coast to coast. Through its website and newsletter, it encourages other communities to take action, to share their innovative initiatives, to network among communities, to foster ongoing intergroup and interfaith dialogue, and to strategize and brainstorm with individuals and groups seeking to stand up to hate in their communities. It is, as the project says, "working together for safe, inclusive communities."

The Public Broadcasting Service recently aired "Not in Our Town: Light in the Darkness," a one-hour documentary focused on the ways that Patchogue, New York, responded to a wave of anti-immigrant violence that culminated in the murder of Marcelo Lucero, an Ecuadorian immigrant who had lived there for 13 years, by seven white youths from nearby communities. The film tracks the call from the Latino community for justice and for the town's grappling with the underlying causes of this violence, the efforts to listen across racial and class lines, and the fragile and slow work of creating a more just and enduring peace.

The Working Group has posted numerous video reports on communities that have done Not in My Town work, including in Kootenai County, Idaho and my hometown, Olympia. A number of institutions of higher education are featured, including Princeton University. And numerous communities and schools have responded to the hate speech of the Westboro Baptist Church, including Charleston and Wheeling, West Virginia, and Gunn High School in the San Francisco Bay Area.

What are some of the factors that mark this growing movement?

One is the fact that a relatively sizeable segment of the community makes a decision to publicly take a stand. Most violence and injustice is sustained by indifference or silence. Here are examples where a decision was made to break this silence and, most powerfully, to align with those who have been traditionally and systemically rejected, excluded or dehumanized. It is one thing for a handful of people to do this. It is quite another for this to become a decision made by the public, especially because it often (though not always) implies a criticism of the existing public order.

Second, the community searches for creative ways to name and embody its opposition to violence and its affirmation of what often becomes a new approach or set of civic relations.

And third, such actions reverse a typical "crowd" dynamic, where the group rallies in favor of the dominant order by scapegoating a person or a group. ("Unanimity minus one," as author Gil Bailie puts it.) Here there is solidarity with the victim or victims but also, in some cases, using creative and nonviolent approaches to defuse the situation.

The Not In My Town movement takes nonviolent action. It does not avoid the violence. It does not accommodate it. It does not use violence to fight violence. Instead, it deploys nonviolence by going public to sound the alarm, by showing solidarity, and by demonstrating for the rest of us what a society might look like where everyone counts.

35

Religious Witness with Homeless People: The Banquet of Justice

March 15, 2012

My brother Larry would have turned 57 today.

In the winter of 2001 he died on the streets. He had spent most of his life on the road—picking fruit, working seasonally cutting Christmas trees, but mostly hitchhiking or riding the rails by clambering into open boxcars before the railway police could spot him. He once told me a harrowing story of scrambling up into the narrow opening between two freight cars and finding a rickety place to stand as the train whipped down the line. Not only was it difficult holding on, he had to avoid getting his leg caught in the steel coupling between the cars. Mostly he succeeded, and when he didn't, he was lucky enough to extract his foot in time to come away with only some bruises and not something worse.

When Larry was thirteen he and a couple friends were arrested for stealing a six-pack of beer. His friends got off, but Larry was rocketed into the juvenile justice system. He spent six weeks in a facility thirty miles from home and was never quite the same afterward. He graduated from high school and feverishly held on to his dream of drumming in a band, but his restlessness and disaffection drove him from place to place, and often into the mean teeth of a society that has little use for poor and homeless people. As one of Kurt Vonnegut's characters in *Slaughterhouse-Five* says, "It's a crime to be poor in America." This is a truth Larry experienced for decades.

He was jailed for vagrancy numerous times and was often physically assaulted. In the 1980s he called me from a mental institution and asked me to get him out—all the drugs they were feeding him, he said, were messing up his head. I talked with the people there, who eventually released him. He came and spent some time with me and we visited a nonprofit that found jobs for poor and low-income people. I was put off by the unexpectedly harsh tone of the staffer with whom we met. I suppose it was some variation on "tough love," but it struck me as unnecessarily shrill and condemning of someone she had just met. Larry took off the next day. I'm one of eight siblings, and each of us over the years offered help, but often Larry's justifiable wariness of the kind of help he experienced at the hands of the system kept him in motion—and on to the next arrest or physical altercation.

For years I wondered why I got involved in political activism. Much of this had to do with the charged atmosphere I experienced in graduate school when a number of powerful social movements were gathering momentum in the 1980s, including those working for a nuclear free future or peace and justice in Central America. But slowly I began to realize that this path was rooted most deeply in a profound poignancy and indignation I felt at the way Larry was treated in this world at every turn: the trauma of systemic disregard, disrespect, and active harassment.

Larry taught me that everyone matters, and it was this primal lesson that consciously and unconsciously fueled a longing within for a world whose policies, structures and conditions reflected this most basic fact.

In 1993, after a decade of activism focused on foreign policy, I worked for several years with Religious Witness with Homeless People (RWWHP). This San Francisco, Calif. coalition of 45 churches, synagogues and mosques, under the leadership of Sr. Bernie Galvin, sought to dismantle the city's Matrix Program. In a city that at the time had 16,000 homeless people and only 1,400 shelter beds, Matrix criminalized sleeping and eating in public. Under this policy, the city police made innumerable arrests and issued tens of thousands of tickets that went unpaid (most homeless people couldn't afford the $78.00 fine) that increasingly risked being converted into jail time.

RWWHP mounted a nonviolent direct action campaign aimed at alerting, educating, winning and mobilizing the populace and policy-makers for change through protests, fasts, and lobbying. We organized a series of sleep-ins in the city's parks, including Union Square (at the heart of the city's fashionable downtown shopping district) and Golden Gate Park when, usually after the late local news signed off for the night, a phalanx of baton-wielding police officers would file in, roust us from our sleeping bags, and haul us off to jail.

We also challenged the ordinance that prohibited eating in public (members of "Food Not Bombs" and other groups had been arrested ladling out soup to hungry people on the street) by organizing a banquet for 800 homeless women and men in the space considered most off-limits by the powers that be: Civic Center Plaza in front of San Francisco's ornate City Hall. A well-planned logistical operation delivered to the site dozens of tables, chairs, linen tablecloths, china, silverware, cut flowers, and many succulent dinner courses. Three choirs provided music. Both concrete and symbolic, this meal was a momentary tableau of the world we longed for: where everyone sits down together, eats together, relaxes together, enjoys one another's company—while disregarding and undoing the regulations designed to separate and diminish.

Faced with the dilemma that this well-publicized feast posed, the police did not swoop down and arrest people from religious communities across the city. Front-page coverage of this event in the local press accelerated the campaign. Eventually RWWHP succeeded in ending the Matrix program, symbolized by the then-district attorney shredding thousands of tickets.

This victory did not mean the end of RWWHP's work. Versions of Matrix have crept up over the past 15 years, and activists have had to mount the ramparts innumerable times in

San Francisco and also across the country. This vital tradition of struggling to end the ongoing attack on homeless human beings is one of the many important tributaries flowing into the river that is the Occupy movement as it readies to renew its work for economic equality.

After Larry died, there was a procession for him organized by the local Catholic Worker and homeless activists. The police tried to prevent us from going into the street, but there was something both gentle and firm in the crowd that changed the atmosphere, a sense of reverence for everyone everywhere as we washed into the streets that Larry loved, even though this was one of the places where he was badgered and arrested and sometimes prevented from occupying. As we moved in a determined silence, the stance of the police shifted. They began to stop traffic so we could move unimpeded through the intersections and on through the downtown area, arriving finally at City Hall, where a few people spoke, imploring the city to do more for those without homes.

I am marking Larry's birthday by remembering his life and death and spirit. His ongoing presence stirs a longing for a time and place where the infinite worth of each one of us is taken for granted—and stokes a willingness to take action to help bring all of us a bit closer to that unending banquet.

36

Quixote Village: Homeless Win Struggle for Permanent Housing

January 3, 2014

In 2007 members of the homeless community in Olympia, Wash., erected a tent city in a downtown parking lot to protest the lack of services and support. Predictably, the city government responded with arrests and shutting down the encampment. That was supposed to be the end of it. Camp Quixote, though, did not disappear. Instead it embarked on a challenging, circuitous journey that at times must have seemed like some 21st century version of the mad misadventures of its visionary namesake, Don Quixote. Now, against all odds, this six-year pilgrimage has paid off, and Camp Quixote has become Quixote Village: an innovative compound of 30 small cottages and a community center. On December 24, the campers moved in — homeless no more.

Nonviolent action is often dismissed as quixotic: utopian, dreamy, pursuing unreachable goals. But this example underscores how idealism is crucial to making real and practical change, though not always in the way one first imagines. The nonviolent resistance that the homeless women and men of Olympia organized did not change city officials' minds, but it prompted allies in the community to come forward. A local church offered space for the encampment, and public support grew. The city was persuaded to pass an ordinance to allow the camp to exist, though with the stipulation that it would have to move every three months. Other churches stepped up, and over the past six years the encampment moved over 20 times.

The vision of the Quixote campers from the beginning was to establish permanent housing, and within a few years the group worked with local allies to establish Panza — a nonprofit organization (named in honor of Don Quixote's more sensible sidekick, Sancho Panza), whose mission would be to build Quixote Village.

Even after land was acquired and a city permit was granted — and necessary funds were raised — business interests in the area went to court to try to stop the project. The court finally ruled in the village's favor, the 30 houses were built and furnished, and now they are occupied and humming with life.

Panza, the village landlord, is leasing the 2.17-acre site from the local county at $1 per year for 41 years. Village residents pay one-third of their income toward rent. Each cottage measures 150 square feet and includes a front porch, garden space and typical utilities. Two were designed to accommodate disabled residents. The community center has a kitchen, laundry facilities, showers, mailboxes and a common area. Bus service is nearby, and the local bus system has donated an eight-passenger van.

Architects met with members of Camp Quixote during the design process, who insisted that the project build freestanding cottages. This input reflects the self-governing nature of the village, where residents "elect officers and decide who lives there based on strict criteria."

"Two years ago, I never thought I'd be here," Quixote Village resident Linda Austin told the *Yakima Herald* after moving into her home. "It gave me a little hope when I thought there was none." In another newspaper story, Austin — who joined Camp Quixote a year ago — touted the transforming impact this experience has had on her: "They basically saved my life – they didn't give up on me... It helped heal my broken spirit."

Quixote Village may offer a model for other locales, so that such a project may not accommodate only 30 people but the millions of people without homes across the United States and beyond. This model has integrated what Gandhi called the obstructive program with the constructive program. Quixote

Village highlights the critical role that nonviolent protest can play in mobilizing people power to challenge what is deemed impossible and to make the breakthroughs necessary for change. At the same time, it underscores the importance of literally building the alternative.

This story is dear to my heart. As someone who grew up in Olympia, I am moved by the emergence of this project and how it carries on the local progressive work for justice — from Rachel Corrie, a local Evergreen College student who was killed nonviolently blockading a bulldozer that was demolishing a family's home in Palestine in 2003 to the movement that organized blockades of arms shipments at the port a few years ago.

Most personal of all is the fact that my brother Larry died on the streets of Olympia as a homeless person a dozen years ago. I vividly imagine Larry sitting on the porch of one of these new cottages, grinning from ear to ear, and then reaching for his snare drum and playing his music, the passion of his life.

"These people have been to hell and back, and some of them several times," Jill Severn, an ally who has been in this struggle since 2007, told the *Seattle Times*.

Now they are home.

37

Keystone XL Pledge of Resistance:
Training for Action

June 21, 2013

In 2015, President Barack Obama decided not to approve the license for the construction of the Keystone XL pipeline. This decision came in the wake of an intensive four-year campaign to scuttle the pipeline. The following essay, written in 2013, focuses on one of the facets of this organizing: The Keystone XL Pledge of Resistance.

"It's time to put our foot down," the retired career Marine said with calm conviction.

He — like the two dozen other women and men who sat together in a downtown Chicago meeting room — had concluded that the accelerating danger of climate change meant he personally had to do something. That's why he and the others had turned up at the Keystone XL Pledge of Resistance nonviolent action training where they spent several hours preparing to risk arrest the following morning at the U.S. State Department's local office. The department, which has jurisdiction in this case because it involves Canada and the United States, is expected to deliver its final recommendation to President Obama on the Keystone XL Pipeline in the next few months. Based on preliminary indications from the department in March, it appears to be leaning toward recommending that the administration approve the pipeline and issue the "presidential permit" which it requires.

The Keystone XL Pipeline — designed to move Canadian tar sands oil through the United States to the Gulf of Mexico — will constitute what former NASA scientist James Hansen has called the "fuse to the biggest carbon bomb on the planet." Approving the pipeline will mean "game over" for the environment, Hansen said, in part because it will signal the lack of U.S. resolve to take the difficult steps required to reverse climate change. Hence the heavy duty organizing over the past two years, including 1,253 people arrested at the White House in 2011, numerous waves of nonviolent resistance, occupations of pipeline routes and construction sites, a million comments on the State Department comments line and, just this week, a clear statement of opposition from ten Nobel peace laureates.

But the people at CREDO Action knew this would not be enough. So this spring they began building a national nonviolent action campaign pegged to the State Department's impending recommendation, with a call for people nationwide to commit themselves to engage in nonviolent civil disobedience if State gives the project a thumbs up. So far, over 62,000 people have taken this pledge, which has given ballast to CREDO's breath-taking vision of "hundreds of peaceful civil disobedience actions" across the nation immediately after the State Department recommends going forward with the pipeline (issuing a "Draft Determination of National Interest") and before the president makes his final decision. (If the president decides against the pipeline, the contingency plans will be tossed and much revelry will no doubt ensue.)

However solemn taking a pledge may be, by itself it mostly tends to devolve into another petition or even a "feel good" exercise. That's why the training phase of this campaign is so important — and impressive. For the past few months, CREDO, Rainforest Action Network and the Other 98% have been putting together a meticulous plan to train hundreds of Pledge of Resistance "action leaders" equipped to organize actions and lead nonviolent action workshops in their own localities. Beginning June 29, they will host weekend-long trainings in 25 cities across the country to prepare action leaders, including in Boston, Tampa, Detroit, Raleigh, Kansas City, Dallas, Albuquerque, Los Angeles, Portland and Seattle. They are free and promise to be content-rich.

177

A recent email from the campaign explains that it has "developed an amazing curriculum which will provide you with the resources and support you need to pull this off — even if you've never done anything like it before."

At the same time, the campaign is organizing a series of small but strategic civil disobedience actions at key sites across the country beforehand to raise the visibility of the campaign, to increase the number of pledge signers, to practice for the large mobilization expected in the fall and, perhaps most importantly, to try to convince the administration that this campaign is real. White House officials have been told that massive civil disobedience will greet a pipeline approval, but they are understandably skeptical. The actions this summer hope to weaken this skepticism — and to increase the possibility that policy-makers will take into account the fact that massive, coordinated, nonviolent resistance could be a plebiscite on this administration's actual commitment to environmental sustainability. The Chicago action was the first of these.

The Sunday training was relatively short but to the point: In four hours it knit together reflection on personal motivation, nonviolence guidelines, campaign briefing, action overview, preparing individual action statements, action role-play, de-escalating tactics and a one-hour legal briefing. The large facilitation team included CREDO's Becky Bonds and Elijah Zarmin, who wrote email blasts for the 2008 Obama presidential campaign; Rainforest Action Network's Amanda Starbucks, Nell Greenberg, Scott Parkin, Abigail Singer and Todd Zimmer, as well as the Other 98%'s Samantha Corbin.

The training was well-organized and facilitated. It was clear that the participants — including those who had never contemplated risking arrest before, which seemed to be the majority of those who attended — felt grounded and prepared for what would happen the next day. I appreciated the opportunity to take part, and I found myself traveling back in time to the first nonviolence trainings I had experienced in the early 1980s. I have since facilitated or co-facilitated scores of them; it had been a long time since I simply participated, and I appreciated the opportunity.

The organizers say that this campaign was inspired by the first Pledge of Resistance, a movement that a few of us started in 1984 in which eventually 100,000 people pledged to engage in nonviolent civil disobedience — and other forms of protest as well — if the United States invaded Nicaragua. There is some evidence that we succeeded in this goal — sources within the Reagan administration indicated to church lobbyists during the summer of 1985 that it backed off from a planned invasion after the imposition of the U.S. embargo on Nicaragua that year was met by 1,000 civil disobedience arrests at federal buildings organized by the Pledge.

Over the next several years, 20,000 pledge signers honored the commitment they made by risking arrest during legislative fights over funding for Nicaraguan rebels and over support for the death-squad government in El Salvador, and many other struggles. The Pledge became an emergency response network that grew accustomed to hitting the streets to clamor for justice and peace in Central America at times of escalations — for example, when the United States, out of the blue, provocatively dispatched 1,800 troops to the Honduran-Nicaraguan border in 1988, or when the six Jesuit priests, their housekeeper and her daughter in San Salvador were brutally assassinated in November 1989. The hundreds of demonstrations that followed this atrocity created the conditions for the United States ending aid to El Salvador and establishing a United Nations-sponsored peace process.

The Keystone XL Pledge of Resistance draws on some of the same dynamics of its predecessor. It has enlisted thousands of people through the simple but powerful medium of promised action. It seeks to prevent a specific policy by increasing its potential political cost. It has a strong commitment to nonviolence (though the word does not appear in the pledge itself) and to nonviolent guidelines. It even uses the term "civil disobedience," which, in some circles these days, is passed over in favor of "civil resistance." I suspect this is because they want to be clear that going to jail is the heart of the campaign.

But there are some new features of the campaign that are also inspiring, including its effective mobilization of social media and its comprehensive approach to training. The original Pledge was highly committed to nonviolent action trainings for both preparation and organizing purposes. In the first months, we led five trainings a week in the San Francisco Bay Area, and continued to offer them on a regular basis after this. We even published a training manual named *Basta! No Mandate for War* that included an annotated, seven-hour training agenda with a series of supporting chapters that anyone could pick up and facilitate with. The Keystone XL Pledge has, however, taken nonviolent action training to the next level. Geared to organizing a large number of civil disobedience actions in a short amount of time, it has crafted an audacious but achievable plan to field hundreds of "action leaders" who, in turn, will be equipped to organize and train others. This will likely prove decisive in determining the success of this effort — and will offer many lessons for future organizing.

On Monday morning, 22 graduates of the Keystone XL Pledge's first training — including the former Marine — were arrested in a disciplined tableau of citizen action, blocking the doors of the State Department's Chicago office and calling on the president to live up to his positions on climate change. With this tune-up over the latest Pledge of Resistance is off and running.

38
School of the Americas Watch: Perseverance Pays Off
December 4, 2013

When the first School of the Americas, or SOA, mass protest was held in 1990, its organizers probably didn't think they would still be at it 23 years later. But enduring social change typically takes many years or decades, especially if your goal is to shutter a facility that's a lynchpin of U.S. geopolitics. Just ask groups like Witness Against Torture and the more recent Close Gitmo coalition, which have been conducting a full court press to shut the prison at Guantanamo Bay for over a decade. It remains open in spite of the fact that President Obama's first official act was to mandate its closure within 12 months. That was several years ago.

Recently thousands of people took part in the annual SOA Watch vigil at the gates of Fort Benning in Columbus, Ga., where the SOA — or the Western Hemisphere Institute for Security Cooperation, as it has been renamed — is housed. They journeyed from across North and South America again to continue this nearly quarter-century protest exposing and resisting the training the school provides to troops from Latin America in counter-insurgency, social control, and (according to training manuals that have surfaced) torture and psychological warfare. Over a thousand soldiers and police officers from Latin America continue to train there every year. For decades, SOA graduates have committed documented human rights violations from Guatemala to Argentina, including the recent political violence unleashed by the 2009 coup in Honduras led by former SOA trainee Romeo Vásquez.

Over the years, several of my colleagues at Pace e Bene have made their opposition to these facts clear by crossing the SOA

181

fence and earning six-month prison sentences, including former training associate Judith Kelly; former program coordinator Laura Slattery, a West Point graduate who hung her army jacket on the fence before crossing over; and Friar Louie Vitale, who has served two half-year jail terms. Pace e Bene folks have also led nonviolence trainings at the annual November gathering.

This year was my first time actually attending the vigil. With a helicopter hovering above, several thousand of us slowly marched to the gates, many bearing crosses with the names of those slain in past and present war zones spanning Central and South America. After a reader on the stage somberly pronounced each name, the assembled responded with one voice: "Presente!"— which is to say, *she is with us, he is remembered, she lives despite the utter effacement that thrums at the heart of torture and assassination, despite the determination of systems of violence and domination to crush resistance and to blot out, disappear and expunge the resister.*

There was a lilting, implacable fierceness in this call and response as we moved to the gates, and then processed past them. The time for speeches was past. The time for preparation was over — the nuts and bolts of organizing, the speaking tours drumming up support, the travel arrangements, the numerous workshops held nearby on Friday and Saturday. Now we were touching the heart of the matter, fusing the hyper-real (those were real soldiers, that was a real helicopter, there was a real training facility over across that fence) with the symbolic in a journey knitting together the living and the dead — past and present, violence and nonviolence. We were recommitting ourselves to the concretely transcendent goal of closing the SOA, and all the SOAs everywhere.

The procession wheeled back toward the gate a second time. Now we stopped and planted the thousands of crosses on the fence, reframing Fort Benning's portal as a place of memorial, mourning and witness — but also, strangely, of renewal. Sober grief unexpectedly gave way to dancing, as if to say that the very act of resistance shakes us free from immobility and despair, freeing up a new sense of hope. Hope not simply for some far-off future when all the SOAs no longer exist, but for the present, as we conspire and stand against the mechanics of terror *now*.

The first mass protest at SOA in 1990 was sparked by the assassination of six Jesuit priests, their housekeeper and her daughter in El Salvador on Nov. 16, 1989. At the time, I was working in Washington, D.C., as part of the U.S. Central America peace movement. Many of us who were part of the movement and living in Washington took part that evening in a hastily organized service at a Jesuit parish in the shadow of the U.S. Capitol. Amid the shock and grief that washed over us that night, there was a renewed determination to dramatically increase nonviolent resistance to the policies that led to such carnage. A thousand demonstrations took place nationally over the next few weeks, and a year later Roy Bourgeois inaugurated the SOA Vigil and Action. Bourgeois was a Maryknoll priest who had already spent 18 months in prison for climbing a tree on the grounds of Fort Benning and broadcasting a tape recording of Archbishop Oscar Romero's words calling on Salvadoran soldiers to lay down their arms.

Despite nearly a quarter of a century of resistance, the school remains open. One might ask: Has the annual event in Columbus simply become a routinized ritual like many other pilgrimages — personally powerful but not necessarily making the larger impact that it seeks?

Perhaps. But it is bracing to see all the approaches SOA Watch has in motion.

In addition to the annual vigil in Georgia, it has also staged a spring demonstration in Washington, D.C., aimed at bolstering its lobbying of Congress, urging it to end the funding for the school. This past April, SOA Watch organized a national phone-in that flooded Congressional offices with calls and staged demonstrations in the city, including a die-in near the Capitol.

183

As a result of an SOA Watch lawsuit, a federal judge ordered the Pentagon to release the names of SOA graduates — this after a long struggle that included Congress adding an amendment to a defense authorization bill that demanded the Department of Defense to release the names.

SOA Watch has built powerful relationships with activists throughout Latin America, including in Honduras, where it had a delegation of observers on the ground during the recent election there.

Most significantly of all, SOA Watch has systematically lobbied Latin American governments to refuse to send their troops to the SOA. In 2012, Ecuador and Nicaragua joined Argentina, Uruguay, Bolivia and Venezuela in deciding to stop sending their personnel there.

All of these gains are rooted in and energized by the power of the annual November mobilization. As the SOA Watch website notes, this movement will continue to mobilize because silence is not an option, because justice has not been rendered and it must be demanded, and because the foundations of this violence must be dismantled.

39

Witness Against Torture:
Making Guantánamo History

January 17, 2014

The National Museum of American History in Washington, D.C., is the repository of the nation's story. While it has spotlighted some of the country's struggles for justice in its permanent collection and temporary exhibits — including an occasional focus on U.S. movements for civil rights, labor, disabilities and peace — much has been left out. One omission has been the ongoing struggle to end torture and indefinite confinement at the U.S. Naval base at Guantánamo Bay, Cuba. Recently Witness Against Torture and other groups sought to correct this by installing a temporary exhibit of its own.

Since 2007, Witness Against Torture, or WAT, has organized annual nonviolent actions every January in Washington to mark the opening of Guantánamo. The group calls for an end to torture, the closure of the prison and the release of or due process for the inmates there. This year, WAT organized a week of thought provoking actions beginning January 6, including at the Supreme Court, Union Station and the Kennedy Center for the Performing Arts.

Witness Against Torture appeared at the museum recently. Supported by 150 activists who had marched from the White House — and by two banners unfurling from an upper balcony emblazoned with the message, "Make Guantánamo History" —a now-familiar tableau appeared at the far end of the museum's cavernous atrium: Men and women in orange jumpsuits and black hoods, the garb of the detainees held at the U.S. prison, sitting or standing in stress positions. The WAT curator introduced the exhibit to the throngs of visitors, and then a song washed through the hall with this recurring refrain: "We're going to tell the nation/No torture/No more."

An Occupy movement-style "mic-check" ensued, with the booming phrases of the speaker repeated by the assembled. With an almost liturgical call-and-response cadence, the story of Guantánamo was told: After over a dozen years, 155 men are still being held; 124 have never been charged; 76 have been cleared for release and are still there. The message was clear: The nation must recognize that this is part of our recent history, must see it as part of our story and must be addressed.

A powerful double meaning was unmistakable. To "make Guantánamo history" involves bringing its violence into the light — to illuminate that it is an ongoing aspect of U.S. policy that must not be ignored or forgotten but seen clearly for what it is. In short, to recognize that it is part of our history. But "making this policy history," of course, also means ending this policy — relegating it to the past once and for all.

This double meaning was also conveyed in the second part of WAT's exhibition, which was staged at the same time in front of the "Price of Freedom: Americans at War" exhibit on the museum's third floor. As organizers explained, the intention was "to revise this exhibit to include twelve years of torture and indefinite detention as the bitter cost of the United States' misguided pursuit of 'national security.' In a booming chorus, members of Witness Against Torture and other groups read from a statement that closed with the lines: 'To honor freedom and justice and the struggles of Americans for these things, we must end torture, close the prison and make Guantánamo history.'"

While WAT curator Carmen Trotta spoke, a security guard rushed up and yanked the hoods from the participants. Security began closing down the exhibit and moving people downstairs.

Then the unexpected happened.

The head of security and a National Parks Police officer appeared. Rather than dispersing the WAT people — and, as expected, arresting them — they discussed the situation with Trotta. They said the group could stay until closing time, some four hours later, as long as they agreed to leave when the museum closed, remain peaceful — and would answer the questions of visitors! There is a powerful video of this exchange, and Carmen's face is a mixture of disbelief and gratitude. He immediately agreed to the conditions and he shook hands with the men. The exhibit proceeded until the museum closed.

It is easy to imagine the outcome going very differently. The fact that WAT's action was allowed to continue was likely due to a mix of factors, including the determined but nonviolent presence of the participants; the larger group of supporters; and a calculation that the decorum of the museum was more likely to be maintained by accommodating this "new temporary exhibit" than by evicting it. But perhaps the museum let this play out because it recognized that WAT's drama is an example of the very thing it exists to document. Dissent had made its way into the museum itself, and the facility ultimately found a way to recognize and even welcome it. Who knows — a permanent exhibit might open on Witness Against Torture one day.

Marie Shebeck, my colleague at Pace e Bene Nonviolence Service, actively participated in this week of action. She was moved by the participatory democracy on display, where everyone's ideas were valued and the actions grew organically out of this sharing. This inclusive process went into building the witness at the museum, with its design, as Marie put it, "to bring the men's stories into the public space. We chose this museum because that's where people go to learn about American history, but Guantánamo is not talked about there. We wanted to do something creative — with songs, visuals and a mic-check — to help the reality of Guantánamo to become part of American culture."

Witness Against Torture — and, in an unexpected way, the National Museum of American History — has taken another step in this direction.

40

Catholic Workers: Sandstorm in Minnesota

February 17, 2014

First it was tea. Then it was salt. Now it's sand.

Successful nonviolent action often hinges on fusing the transcendent with the everyday. While it frames the struggle in visionary terms like "justice," it does so in ways that we can touch, feel, see and experience up close. So, for example, the civil rights movement's lunch counter sit-ins in the 1960s indissolubly linked the trans-historical crime of racism with the need all of us have to eat three times a day, driving home monumental injustice in terms most people could viscerally grasp: an obstacle to straightforwardly meeting the most basic of human needs.

American revolutionaries got the point across about their British overlords by pitching a colonial staple into Boston harbor. Gandhi shook the same imperial system 150 years later by illegally making salt. Both cases pointed out the crises of their time by using material both highly symbolic but also utterly at hand, thus managing to transform an often abstract and elusive form of oppression, the overarching machinery of empire, into a reality that people could touch — and, by touching, change.

Now, sand has entered the mix.

Recently 30 people were found guilty in a Winona, Minn. courtroom of trespassing at two local facilities where silica sand used in hydraulic fracking is processed and transported. Stemming from a nonviolent action organized by the Winona Catholic Worker and others from throughout the Midwest, a four-day jury trial kept the original protest alive by trying to put "frac sand" on trial. Judge Jeffrey Thompson imposed a sentence of fines, court costs and probation.

Silica sand is a necessary component of fracking, which reportedly uses 10,000 tons of silica sand to frack a single well. Wisconsin is the biggest producer of frac sand, with hundreds of mines. Winona, located near the Wisconsin border and the Mississippi River, has become a key transshipment point, with about 100 trucks carrying thousands of tons of sand crossing the city daily.

If the Sandman's job, as legend has it, is to put us to sleep, a growing movement in Minnesota and Wisconsin has taken up the opposite task: wiping the sleep from our eyes. They have done so through concerted outreach to the city council and the larger community aimed at raising the visibility of the immediate and long-term consequences of both fracking and the sand that makes it possible, including the impacts that harmful silica sand emissions pose to human health. As *Inside Climate News* reports: "The extent and effect of pollution from mining, processing and transporting frac sand is only partially understood. The biggest concern is the release of extra-tiny dust matter called PM 2.5, which are 2.5 micrometers in diameter and can penetrate lung tissue and enter the bloodstream."

The movement to end the burgeoning frac sand industry has organized a growing series of public events, with the April 2013 blockade being the largest to date. Just before that action, organizer Diane Leutgeb-Munson laid out why people had decided to take this action, including risking arrest. "We will not be complicit in the hydraulic fracturing industry, known for poisoning water and land across the country," she said. "We will not stand by and watch our landscape be forever altered. If there is no other way to stop this from happening, we will simply stand in the way."

That morning people stood in the way at two sites. Half the group assembled at the CD Corporation at the Winona Port Authority, where sand is loaded onto barges and then shipped down the Mississippi. Eighteen people nonviolently blocked trucks there, preventing them from unloading sand for about an hour. The others headed to a nearby sand washing and processing facility. Seventeen people occupied the driveway, shutting it down for two hours. Thirty-five people were charged with trespass. They finally had their day in court earlier this month.

A trial of this kind is unusual for Winona, as judged by the glut of local print and TV media attention it garnered, with many local news outlets reporting every day on the proceedings. The *Winona Daily News* led off its coverage of the trial's first day this way: "The charge is misdemeanor trespass, but there's no question that sand mining, hydraulic fracking and the international petrochemical industry are at the heart of what is easily the largest and most political trial in recent Winona history. Monday was not a typical day at the county courthouse."

Defendant Steve Clemons posted a blog each day of the trial. Meanwhile, all 30 defendants were given an opportunity to give testimony. On the concluding day, for example, Mike Miles testified that he found himself "walking up driveways I shouldn't have because of my commitment to nonviolence." He knew if he got arrested he would have his "day in court and hopefully be able to tell the truth, the whole truth, to a jury serving as the conscience of the community," a not so oblique reference to the fact that the judge had throughout the trial repeatedly squashed any attempt by the defense to address the motivation and intent of the action. When asked by the defense attorney why he risked arrest, Miles said he was motivated by the urgency of the crisis facing us, declaring "we must do everything within our power [to try to prevent or mitigate climate change]."

Peaceable civil disobedience is warranted when every other remedy for change has been exhausted. But it is also warranted in response to an emergency, even if every mechanism for change hasn't been used. Indeed, it becomes a powerful tool by helping to both interrupt the harm in question and by alerting, educating and mobilizing the population to demand an end to that harm. In his testimony, Miles got at the necessity to respond to the escalating emergency of the climate crisis. He and his community could not wait. Willfully trespassing to save a baby in a house that is on fire is justified, or so the argument goes. In this case, the sand is headed to the next fracking well and they had to prevent the harm in the making.

And so the community was alerted. A Wisconsin-Minnesota coalition is working on frac sand; the Winona City Council is considering establishing frac sand emissions monitors; and a few miles from Winona on the Wisconsin side of the Mississippi River, a local school district has just announced a legal battle to oppose the Glacier Sands truck-to-rail frac sand facility that's proposed to be located across from one of its schools.

My friend Marie Shebeck was among those arrested and convicted in this case. She was deeply moved by the action and its process. "Many of the participants were from Winona or had ties to it, and the rest of us were invited by the Winona community to take this action," Shebeck said. "When forming the action, we reflected deeply on what it means to care for creation. And now that the trial is over, there is the sense that this effort is going to continue."

41

The Anti-Drone Movement:
Renouncing the Right to Bear Drones

September 13, 2013

Reports about the use of chemical weapons in Syria has sparked worldwide revulsion. Horror at such atrocities has its roots in World War I's searing plumes of mustard gas that decimated thousands of troops and that still swirl through the trenches of our collective mind. But it is also grounded in our conscious or unconscious memory of every pivotal moment in the history of war when one combatant's edge widened incrementally or dramatically over another with the latest innovation in killing.

The ability of new weaponry to mechanize and geometrically multiply casualties with every turn of the technological wheel has proven chillingly advantageous to systems of domination. But this superiority has not only been numerical. Its power often has laid in its capability to deface and ultimately obliterate the facticity and stubbornly human presence of the other — whether it be with the meat grinding Gatling gun of the Civil War or the vaporous immensity of the atomic bomb. Virtually every new weapon over the past 5,000 years has not only been designed to defeat the opponent with greater firepower but to reduce, ruin and extinguish her or his body, presence, physical integrity — the qualities that makes us irreducibly human.

We are now in the midst of the drones revolution, the next leap in technologized lethality. The quantitative horror that drones have ushered into the world is deeply troubling. For example, U.S. drones have killed an estimated 3,149 people in Pakistan since 2004. At the same time a qualitative horror rumbles through our collective consciousness rooted in the growing capacities of drones, including their radical particularity, universal comprehensiveness, and increasing automation.

The precision of drones has dramatically refashioned the concept of most battlefield weapons, which steadily have increased the ability to kill large numbers of people. A military drone, on the contrary, is hyper-personal, designed and tailored to kill a particular person. While the United States regularly carries out what it terms signature strikes — aimed at classes of people that are presumed to be terrorists because they match a certain demographic profile (young men, for example) — the stark reality of drones is that they are designed to track and eliminate specific individuals.

Paradoxically, this very particularity makes the potential reach of drones universal. One by one, we are all hypothetically at risk. Any one of us could find ourselves on a "kill list" if we are deemed by "deemers" to fit the system's criteria at any given moment. As the NSA revelations of Edward Snowden and others have underscored, the capacity increasingly exists for the U.S. government and other entities to amass profiles on every human being on the planet. Perhaps all seven billion of us are on a master list whereby the "deemer-in-chief" can toggle us from the "non-kill list" to the "kill list" when national security demands it. Whether this is the case or not, the growing capacity of drones to roam the planet to track and eliminate targets drawn from a comprehensive super-database is a prospect with which we must grapple going forward.

Even more than this, there is the possibility that such a comprehensive system will become virtually automated. Not only might there be a universal list, it could be activated and maintained by a set of algorithms, freeing those glued to the monitors and working the joysticks at places like Creech Air Force Base in Nevada — as well as their bosses who now compile and sign off on the lists — from the sometimes PTSD-inducing task of deciding who will live and who will die.

All these facets of drones — customizable killing, planet-wide surveillance and targeting, and the potential for them to be the lynchpin of a self-regulating, ubiquitous and permanent military regime — increase lethality but also degrade, destroy and erase the inviolable human presence.

The drones revolution is on, and every effort is being made to get us to enlist. Over the past few years this has included an unrelenting touting that drones are a foregone conclusion. Virtually every day there are new revelations in the press — for example, the Defense Advanced Research Projects Agency recently announced that it was working on underwater drones, and there seems to be a thriving "do-it-yourself " drones industry — while U.S. drone warfare continues apace in the Middle East and the Horn of Africa. (Although most analysts downplay the role drones might play in Syria if the United States goes in, this spring a news account detailed how the CIA has plans to carry out drone attacks against extremists in the Syrian opposition.) This is a new form of subtle and not-so-subtle conscription, designed not so much to fill the ranks of the armed services as to gradually get us to assume that a drone-run world is normal, good and just another part of the future.

But there is resistance to this "cultural draft," including the movement that, for the past few years, has been growing and broadening. (In reflecting on this movement, I recently explored the idea of promulgating an international treaty banning drones, inspired by the international treaty banning land mines.) Anti-drone protests have been staged in Yemen and Britain. CodePink has been building an increasingly powerful anti-drones campaign, And recently, the "Beale 5" were sentenced in a Sacramento, Calif., courtroom for a nonviolent civil disobedience action they engaged in on October 30, 2012 at Beale Air Force Base in Northern California, which provides surveillance drones that scout locations for killer drones. They were convicted of trespassing at the base after a day-long bench trial, where they faced a maximum sentence of six months in federal prison and a $5,000 fine. Judge Carolyn Delaney sentenced the five — Janie Kesselman, Sharon Delgado, Shirley Osgood, Jan Hartsough and David Hartsough — to 10 hours of community service after the defendants told her that they would rather go to jail than accept fines or probation.

In her statement before the judge, Jan Hartsough, who was a Peace Corps volunteer in Pakistan in the mid-1960s, said:

> After living and working there for two years, Pakistan is a part of me. I have followed with great pain and sadness the drone attacks on Pakistanis. I have learned from Pakistani victims of drone strikes that they are experiencing psychological trauma — never knowing when a drone might strike again. Kids are afraid to go to school; adults are afraid to gather for a funeral or a wedding celebration for fear of becoming a "target." ... So what have we accomplished with our drone attacks? When will we wake up and see that there are much better ways to win the respect of the world's people? As a mother and grandmother I seek to find ways to help create a more peaceful world for future generations. Ending drone warfare is a concrete step we can and must take.

After the statements of Hartsough and the others, the judge declared that prison would serve "no purpose."

42

Seattle and WTO:
Rereading the Lessons for Today
February 9, 2012

The acrid fumes of tear-gas hung in the air as a young woman, her face swathed in black fabric, readied to heave a newspaper box through the plate-glass window of the Nike Store.

It was the afternoon of November 30, 1999 and the "Battle of Seattle" was on. Tens of thousands of people had traveled from across the globe to the Northwest United States to protest the World Trade Organization Ministerial Conference, which was on track to reinforce the injustice of corporate globalization and the perils it posed to indigenous societies, labor standards, human rights, civil liberties and the environment.

I had been asked by Global Exchange (a San Francisco-based organization that has long been a proponent of fair trade) to join in as a peacekeeper during the multi-day protest. Moving through the increasingly chaotic streets, I spotted the woman with her conscripted newspaper box and, just before she hoisted it through the glass, I trotted over and asked her what she was doing.

For the next half-hour, we had a heart-to-heart.

She shared her anguish at the violence of Indonesian sweatshops that produced Nike shoes. In the light of that injustice, smashing a window counted as nothing. In fact, from her perspective, it was a good thing—it would directly identify the company as a human rights violator and would challenge business as usual. Most of all, it would help panic the powers that be into changing things in the face of this growing unrest.

It has been over a dozen years so I don't remember verbatim everything I shared with my impromptu conversation partner, but it was something like this.

I let her know that the two of us were in agreement about this injustice and that it must be challenged and stopped. This is why I had traveled to Seattle—and why, for 15 years, I had been part of movements working for justice. To me, though, there was a better way than property destruction to achieve this goal—and the 70,000 people marching that week in Seattle were illustrating it.

Gathered from around the planet, they were dramatizing a growing movement for change using nonviolent people power. These thousands were alerting and educating the public in a way, from my perspective, that violent action would not. Violent action will not panic the power-holders but it will push away the general populace. Power-holders, in fact, love it, because it gives them an excuse to delegitimize and destroy movements. In the end, social change depends not on creating the sense of chaos and social disorder, but on mobilizing the populace to remove its support for such injustice and to exercise people-power for change.

As we talked, she put down the box. She did not hurl it through the window and eventually she melted back into the crowd. Then, when I went off to engage another person poised to hurl a different newspaper box through a window further down the block, someone else scooped up the first one and pitched it through the window.

Bandana-clad activists (estimated at only 100 to 200 people) managed to break enough windows and spray-paint enough buildings to dislodge the primary focus from the police rampage in the morning to the image of marauding anonymous activists wreaking chaos throughout downtown Seattle in the afternoon.

The criminal behavior of the police—in which thousands of peaceful protesters, sitting in the streets outside the convention hall where we engaged in nonviolent civil disobedience, were shot indiscriminately at close range by rubber bullets and blinded for a time by relentless waves of tear-gas (for which the City of Seattle years later paid out financial settlements to some protesters)—exposed the violence that the state will inflict to protect injustice. Now, however, this narrative had to share the stage with a competing one. Hence the frame that ultimately prevailed: "The Battle of Seattle." After all, it takes two sides to make a skirmish.

In Seattle, an ambiguity was built into the action itself. We were told at a pre-action gathering the night before that the organizers had just decided that the nonviolence guidelines would be in force only until 2:00 p.m., after which they would not apply. And almost to the minute, this is what transpired: the window smashing, the spray-painting, and the clashes with the police began like clockwork in the early afternoon.

The WTO protest was a watershed event, which was immediately noticed by the press. "Protest's power to alter public awareness," read the December 3 headline of the *San Jose Mercury News*, while the December 5 edition of the *Los Angeles Times* declared, "WTO is Humbled, Changed Forever by Outside Forces." It definitively put the hazards of globalization on the social radar screen.

This success was due predominantly, from my point of view, to the nonviolent and creative people power of the mobilization and not to the attention-getting property destruction of a handful of activists. In fact, had the police not engaged in their even more media-genic violence (made all the more glaring by the fact that it was launched, not as a reaction to protest violence, but as a first-strike against peaceful demonstrators), the WTO protest would have likely been assessed very differently.

Unfortunately, though, the wrong lessons have often been drawn from the Seattle mobilization. In the anti-globalization and other movements since then, Seattle has often inspired strategies that provide ample wiggle room on property destruction and even what amounts to street-fighting, enshrined in the now famous "diversity of tactics" principle.

Which brings us to the conversation we are having in 2012 about violence and nonviolence in the Occupy movement.

In sorting out the two tendencies at the heart of the present discussion—"nonviolent people power" and "diversity of tactics"—it is helpful to see how they share at least three points of agreement:

- Social change is imperative
- The goal is justice
- Powerful action is key

They diverge, however, on the question of how each of these is achieved. From my perspective, enduring social change does not flow most effectively from violence-generated social disorder. Such action is typically seized on by power-holders to destroy movements and it often frightens or alienates the public. This seems to be borne out by much of the recent work of Erica Chenoweth and others that quantify how violent campaigns are often much less successful than nonviolent ones.

Instead, social change (as social movement activist and theorist Bill Moyer writes in his book *Doing Democracy*) flows from social movement that builds nonviolent people power. "Social movements," according to Moyer, "are collective actions in which the populace is alerted, educated, and mobilized, over years and decades, to challenge the power-holders and the whole society to redress social problems or grievances and restore critical social values." In short, this means removing the pillars of support for injustice, including the direct or indirect support of the populace and often other economic, political, cultural, or media pillars. Nonviolent action is more likely to nurture this process because:

- It maintains a focus on the issue rather than the violence/counter violence cycle;
- It is more likely to raise the visibility of both the injustice being challenged and the justice that it seeks.
- Violent action is more likely to obscure the issue and the outcome it is working for; and
- When nonviolent action is met by violence, the focus is likely to remain both on the issue and on the violence of the state, which can increase rather than decrease public support for change.

But the effectiveness of such nonviolent action often depends on the third point of agreement: the need for powerful action.

Those supporting violent tactics often feel that nonviolent action is not powerful—and, truth be told, it is often not as powerful as it could be. Nonviolent action needs to be commensurate with the injustice one is struggling to change—which means that it needs to powerfully accomplish its goals, including dramatizing the fundamental need for change; illuminating a vision of the alternative; inviting the public to re-think this issue; and offering concrete steps for people to withdrawing consent from the status quo and to support a more life-giving alternative.

The good news is that it can be this powerful.

This power depends on creativity, clarity, strategic planning, training, discipline, execution, interpretation, and follow-up. The Occupy movement itself is a good example of this. When it has maintained a nonviolent spirit, it has been an effective and historic force for highlighting the problem of inequality and laying the groundwork for being a force for change. Its scattered violent actions, however, have been less powerful than its nonviolent ones, because they have often muddied the issue and reframed the conversation from inequality to the violence of Occupiers. This has likely cost support for the movement within Occupy and among the larger populace.

For those of us who are committed to nonviolence in challenging massive and structural inequity, the answer is not to demonize those who are committed to a variety of approaches, including violent ones. We are called to relentless dialogue with those with whom we disagree—as I attempted to do on the streets of Seattle twelve years ago. Most importantly, we are called to build a movement that demonstrates the power and effectiveness of nonviolent people power.

In the end, this will be more effective than all the arguments in the world.

43

The National Council of Elders:
Collective Wisdom

August 16, 2012

One of the breathtaking features of the last 50 years has been the vast outpouring of nonviolent people power. While there is no denying the endless parade of horrors over the intervening decades, powerful movements have invariably sprung up to challenge them one by one. Struggles for equality, freedom, democracy, peace and sustainability in innumerable contexts — unleashing dizzying displays of creativity and relentless persistence — have not allowed this violence to go unchecked. Many of these efforts have changed the political or social landscape by putting a dent in the long-entrenched architecture of oppression and vowing to come back for more.

How did this unique tidal wave of social change get rolling? What sustained it? How did one movement inspire another? Why did they appear when they did? Were they part of a trans-historical shift? When a historian sits down to write the definitive history of the 20th century in a hundred years or so, she will likely grapple with these questions more clearly than we can. From that trans-generational vantage point, she may be better equipped — by distance, hindsight and algorithms we can't yet imagine — to discern the significance of the immense web of connections between innumerable struggles for emancipation across the globe that took off beginning in the middle of the last century.

For us, though, we mostly look through a glass darkly. We get suggestive clues from books like Paul Hawken's *Blessed Unrest*, where he tracks a sprawling though still largely unnoticed mega-movement for change percolating across the planet, and the online Global Nonviolent Action Database. Nevertheless, since we're still firmly in the midst of the hurtling fluorescence of the Big Bang unleashed by Rosa Parks all those years ago, it's still hard to truly appreciate just how world-historical this political, economic and cultural turn has been.

Every so often, though, we manage to get a clear glimpse.

The vivid example of this was the recent launch of the National Council of Elders in Greensboro, North Carolina. The brainchild of James Lawson, Philip Lawson and Vincent Harding — who all played powerful roles in the U.S. Civil Rights movement — the council includes "leaders from many of the defining American social justice movements of the 20th century, committed to educating and mentoring future leaders who will join and lead democratizing movements in the 21st century." As the *Madison Times* reported about the gathering:

> They come from all walks of the civil and human rights struggle, each a distinguished leader with a long record of advocacy, molded in courage and sacrifice. But last week, these leaders — some in their 60s, 70s, and even a few at age 80 and beyond — came together from across the nation in what they called "an historic gathering" at North Carolina A&T University, to be reborn in a collective purpose, amid the legacy of the 1960 lunch counter sit-in movement that inspired the world.

At one point the council assembled under a statue depicting the Greensboro Four, the group whose historic sit-in at the local Woolworth's touched off powerful desegregation actions throughout the South and beyond. The photograph is riveting. Beside the iconic founders are Dolores Huerta, who cofounded the United Farm Workers with César Chávez; Mel White, who founded Soulforce, which works for LGBT equality; Dorothy Cotton, a key organizer with the Southern Christian Leadership Conference; Dr. Gwendolyn Zoharah Simmons, an activist in the

Student Nonviolent Coordinating Committee and later an American Friends Service Committee staffer; Bernice Johnson Reagon, a founder of the musical group, Sweet Honey in the Rock; Joyce Johnson and Nelson Johnson, founders of the Beloved Community in Greensboro; Arthur Waskow, founder of the Shalom Center; John Fife, who cofounded the Sanctuary movement as part of the Central America peace movement; and Louie Vitale, my co-worker and friend, a founder of the Nevada Desert Experience and Pace e Bene. Other members include Marian Wright Edelman, founder of the Children's Defense Fund; Grace Lee Boggs, lifelong social activist in Detroit; George Tinker, prominent American Indian activist; and theologian Sr. Joan Chittister, O.S.B., a long-time peace and human rights advocate.

The group calculated that those assembled represented over 1,250 years of social activism.

While there is much focus in the National Council of Elders on the past and sharing its members' legacies, the elders were not simply handing on the baton to the next generation. In preparation for the gathering, members were asked to name both what they are doing now as well as what they did in the 20th century. Most of them are as actively involved as ever in the ongoing project of making the world a better place. As Nelson Johnson said at the group's press conference, "The past is a way of equipping us for the future and we ain't in no way tired yet."

Conclusion

In the early 1980's I joined the peace movement because of the issues—but I stayed because of the people. I was perennially energized, challenged, and transformed by the many women and men I was fortunate to meet in innumerable meetings and mobilizations. I got to meet and take action with countless people who came to embody creativity and humor, courage and wisdom, grief and joy as they grappled with the implacable challenges facing our relationships, families, communities and societies.

I learned something from all of them.

In these pages we have reflected on scores of human beings who have wagered that they have the power to make change. In most cases, they did not plan this as their life's work. Life, and its deeply embedded challenges, intervened, and they found themselves swerving in the direction of a world where everyone counts. This is not easy. There are many set-backs. But many came to see that obstacles were an inherent part of the job, and often summoned the power to surmount them, or at least to give everything in trying.

One of the biggest lessons many discovered is that we cannot change the world by ourselves. If we take the burden of the world entirely on our shoulders, we will likely be destroyed by it. We need other beautiful, cranky, vulnerable, and committed people to do this. We need mentors. We need affinity groups. We need organizations. We need community. To lift up particular change-makers is not to isolate them or to put them out of reach, but, instead, to honor what they brought to the circles they were part of that ultimately mobilized creativity and transformation.

Each of these change-makers has wholeheartedly thrown themselves into the work for the healing of the world—and so can we. César Chávez, Wangari Maathai, Vincent Harding and everyone in this book is extending a hand to us, and welcoming us to the powerful process of imagining and designing and building a more nonviolent and just society, of crafting and nourishing a culture of active nonviolence.

Will we take their hand? Will we answer their call?

In April 1967, Dr. Martin Luther King, Jr., delivered a pivotal call to end the Vietnam War. The words of this historic speech— drafted by Vincent Harding—resound across the decades and deliver a call to all of us to grapple with today's monumental challenges:

> We are now faced with the fact that tomorrow is today. We are confronted with the fierce urgency of now. In this unfolding conundrum of life and history there is such a thing as being too late. Procrastination is still the thief of time...We must move past indecision to action. ...Now let us begin. Now let us rededicate ourselves to the long and bitter — but beautiful — struggle for a new world. ...Shall we say the odds are too great?... Or will there be another message, of longing, of hope, of solidarity...whatever the cost? The choice is ours, and though we might prefer it otherwise we must choose in this crucial moment of human history.

In this spirit, each of the voices in this book is inviting us to engage and transform the violence and injustice that roils all around us at this historic moment – and to join the movement for justice, peace and healing in our lives, in our families, in our communities, in our societies, and in our wounded and sacred world.

WAGING NONVIOLENCE
PEOPLE-POWERED NEWS & ANALYSIS

Most of the essays in this book were first published by *Waging Nonviolence*, a leading source for news, analysis and original reporting about social movements around the globe. They tell in-depth, compelling stories about how ordinary people are building power every day with nonviolent strategies and tactics in their struggles against repressive regimes and for social, economic and environmental justice — reshaping our world in the process.

Since 2009, their vibrant media platform has been devoted to fostering a more sophisticated conversation in the mainstream media about nonviolent action. It also serves as a meeting place for people interested in deepening their understanding of people-powered movements, and for activists to share ideas and analysis so that they can be more effective in their efforts to build a more just and peaceful world.

wagingnonviolence.org
facebook.com/wagingnonviolence
@wagingnv

207

Pace e Bene / Peace and Goodness

*Together we can imagine, create, and live a different way
and a different world*

Pace e Bene Nonviolence Service explores ways to tap the power of
peace and goodness to make a difference in our lives, our
communities, and our world through:

Nonviolent Education

Pace e Bene's nonviolence workshops, trainings, and study groups
provide concrete ways to grapple with the challenges we face and to
inspire effective action. Pace e Bene has led over 800 workshops
worldwide on the power of creative nonviolence to transform
relationships and to engage societies.

Pace e Bene's publications, website, and speaking events
increase awareness of the core values and methods of creative
nonviolence to discover positive alternatives to violence and passivity
and to support the emergence of a culture of nonviolent options.

Nonviolent Community

Pace e Bene's growing network
supports individuals and organizations applying nonviolent methods
for personal and social transformation. Pace e Bene seeks to promote
the growth of nonviolent communities and the emergence of a
nonviolent culture.

Nonviolent Action

*Pace e Bene's programs offer individuals and organizations a process for
taking concrete steps for nonviolent change.*
Pace e Bene collaborates with organizations and movements that
challenge the cycle of violence; foster just and lasting peace;
champion human rights; confront the violence of poverty and all
forms of oppression; and strengthen spiritually-based initiatives for a
better world. In 2014 they launched Campaign Nonviolence a long-
term movement to build a culture of peace and nonviolence free from
war, poverty, racism, the climate crisis, and the epidemic of violence.

www.paceebene.org

Campaign Nonviolence

A national grassroots movement to build a culture of peace and mainstream nonviolence, www.CampaignNonviolence.org.

Campaign Nonviolence is a new national grassroots movement that seeks to mobilize the nation and the world through the power of active nonviolence to help abolish war, poverty, racism, environmental destruction and the epidemic of violence and build a new culture of peace and nonviolence. It seeks a culture that values, promotes, teaches, and applies the power of nonviolent transformation in the face of violence and injustice. It endeavors to take active nonviolence into the mainstream, and challenge the false notion that nonviolence is passive, weak, and ineffective. It works to make the tools of nonviolent transformation accessible to all. It wants to educate every human being in the method, way and wisdom of active nonviolence that one day, war will end, and everyone will live in peace with justice.

Campaign Nonviolence tries to spread the vision, principles and methods of active, creative nonviolence, even as it connects the dots between war, poverty, racism, the climate crisis, and the epidemic of violence. No one of these monumental challenges will be solved separately. They are intimately connected and must be solved in an integral fashion. That's why Campaign Nonviolence invites us not only to connect the dots between the issues, but also to connect the dots between the organizations and movements that have been toiling separately for years for a better world. Campaign Nonviolence envisions an emerging "movement of movements" that joins forces, pools people-power, and works collaboratively in comprehensively addressing these challenges.

But there is more. Campaign Nonviolence insists that resolving these monumental challenges will only happen by unleashing the power of active, creative, liberating and audacious nonviolence. Nonviolence challenges the power and systems of violence through grassroots, bottom up, people power. It disarms, heals, rebuilds, and leads to a more just, more peaceful world, and it does so through just, peaceful means.

We organize marches and public actions for peace, justice and nonviolence each year during the third week of September, around The International Day of Peace, September 21st, as well as hold nonviolence trainings around the nation and promote "Nonviolent Cities."

Campaign Nonviolence calls upon people everywhere to join together in a new grassroots movement against war, poverty, racism, the climate crisis and the epidemic of violence. We call upon Campaign Nonviolence people to practice nonviolence toward themselves, toward all others, and toward the planet, as we reenergize and rebuild a new global grassroots movement of nonviolence for a new world of peace. Together, we can make a difference, and do our part to make a new nonviolent world a reality.

www.CampaignNonviolence.org

Other Books from Pace e Bene Press

Engage

Exploring Nonviolent Living

A program for learning, practicing and experimenting
with nonviolent options for our lives and for a
sustainable, just and peaceful world

We have more power than we think.

Engage can help us tap into that power and equip us to improve our lives, our communities, and our world. Using numerous stories, exercises and resources, The *Engage* Workbook offers us a way to learn, study and practice the nonviolent options available to us. *Engage* provides tools for individuals and groups to take action for justice and peace in the midst of war and injustice. *Engage* is ideal for advocacy organization, campus networks, faith communities, and any group seeking to work together to create a society committed to justice, democracy, peace, sustainability and equality.

Engage, a project of Pace e Bene Nonviolence Service is based on the experience of leading hundreds of workshops. Order a copy of our book, *Engage: Exploring Nonviolent Living*, by Laura Slattery, Ken Butigan, Veronica Pelicaric and Ken Preston at www.paceebene.org.

The Nonviolent Life

By John Dear

From Pace e Bene Press
——to help build——
Campaign Nonviolence

"How can we become people of nonviolence and help the world become more nonviolent? What does it mean to be a person of active nonviolence? How can we help build a global grassroots movement of nonviolence to disarm the world, relieve unjust human suffering, make a more just society and protect creation and all creatures? What is a nonviolent life?"

These are the questions John Dear—Nobel Peace Prize nominee, long time peace activist and Pace e Bene staff member—poses in this ground-breaking book. John Dear suggests that the life of nonviolence requires three simultaneous attributes: being nonviolent toward ourselves; being nonviolent to all people, all creatures, and all creation; and joining the global grassroots movement of nonviolence.

After thirty years of preaching the Gospel of nonviolence, John Dear offers a simple, original yet profound way to capture the crucial elements of nonviolent living, and the possibility of creating a new nonviolent world. According to John, "Most people pick one or two of these dimensions, but few do all three. To become a fully rounded, three dimensional person of nonviolence, we need to do all three simultaneously." Perhaps then he suggests, we can join the pantheon of peacemakers from Jesus and Francis to Dorothy Day and Mahatma Gandhi.

In this book, John Dear proposes a simple vision of nonviolence that everyone can aspire to. It will help everyone be healed of violence, and inspire us to transform our culture of violence into a new world of nonviolence! Order your copy at www.paceebene.org.

LOVE IS WHAT MATTERS
Writings on Peace and Nonviolence

By Friar Louie Vitale, OFM

Foreword by Martin Sheen
Afterword by John Dear
Edited by Ken Butigan

From Pace e Bene Press!

Love is What Matters is a collection of writings on peace and nonviolence by Friar Louie Vitale, a dedicated Franciscan peacemaker and founder of Pace e Bene Nonviolence Service, which works to bring a spiritually grounded practice of active nonviolence through education, resources and action for nonviolent change.

Fr. Louie is a Franciscan priest who has sought to put the vision of peacemaking articulated and practiced by Francis and Clare of Assisi into practice. A former provincial of the St. Barbara Province in the western United States, Vitale was a co-founder of the Nevada Desert Experience—a spiritually-based movement that sought to end nuclear weapons testing at the Nevada Test Site—and Pace e Bene. As a long-time social activist, he has engaged in civil disobedience for nearly four decades in pursuit of peace and justice, and has been arrested more than 400 times.

In this series of short essays written by Vitale over the course of nearly thirty years he recounts his nonviolent striving towards peace and justice to end war, torture, racism, poverty, climate destruction and greed in the spirit of St. Francis of Assisi.

Order your copy at www.paceebene.org.

To order copies of *Nonviolent Lives*
Contact Pace e Bene Nonviolence Service
Phone: 510-268-8765
Email: info@paceebene.org
Website: www.paceebene.org

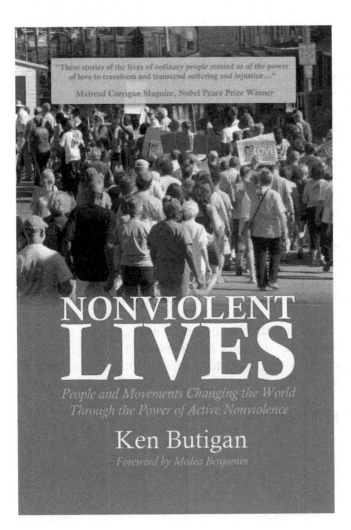

"These stories of the lives of ordinary people remind us of the power of love to transform and transcend suffering and injustice..."

Mairead Corrigan Maguire, Nobel Peace Prize Winner

NONVIOLENT
LIVES

*People and Movements Changing the World
Through the Power of Active Nonviolence*

Ken Butigan

Foreword by Medea Benjamin